Access 2106 Relational Database Design
Student Edition

30 Bird Media
510 Clinton Square
Rochester NY 14604
www.30Bird.com

Access 2016 Relational Database Design
Student Edition

CEO, 30 Bird Media: Adam A. Wilcox

Series designed by: Clifford J. Coryea, Donald P. Tremblay, and Adam A. Wilcox

Managing Editor: Donald P. Tremblay

Writer: Joe Barrett

Instructional Design Lead: Clifford J. Coryea

Instructional Designer: Robert S. Kulik

Keytester: Kurt J. Specht

COPYRIGHT © 2017 30 Bird Media LLC. All rights reserved

No part of this work may be reproduced or used in any other form without the prior written consent of the publisher.

Visit www.30bird.com for more information.

Trademarks

Some of the product names and company names used in this book have been used for identification purposes only and may be trademarks or registered trademarks of their respective manufacturers and sellers.

Disclaimer

We reserve the right to revise this publication without notice.

ACCS2016-RDD-R10-SCB

Table of Contents

Introduction 1
   Course setup 2

Chapter 1: Database fundamentals 3
   Module A: Understanding general database terms 4
   Module B: Relational databases 13
   Module C: Access interface and objects 16

Chapter 2: Database design 23
   Module A: Fundamentals of efficient design 24
   Module B: The normal forms 36
   Module C: Creating and modifying databases 41
   Module D: Relationships and keys 48

Chapter 3: Tables 55
   Module A: Creating tables 56
   Module B: Creating fields 60
   Module C: Data Validation 64
   Module D: Relationships and keys 71

Chapter 4: Queries 81
   Module A: Creating basic queries 82
   Module B: Modifying queries 111
   Module C: Using calculated fields 121

Chapter 5: Forms 131
   Module A: Creating simple forms 132
   Module B: Form design 146
   Module C: Form controls 155

Chapter 6: Reports 173
   Module A: Creating Reports 174
   Module B: Report controls 185
   Module C: Formatting reports 198

Introduction

Welcome to *Access 2016 Relational Database Design*. This course provides the basic concepts and skills to start being productive with Microsoft Access 2016: How to design and create a relational database, navigate the Access interface, and how to create and modify tables, queries, forms, and reports.

You will benefit most from this courses if you want to gain a basic understanding of relational databases and be able to design and build a simple database in Access 2016.

The course assumes you know how to use a computer, and that you're familiar with Microsoft Windows. It does not assume that you've used a different version of Access or another database system before.

After you complete this course, you will know:

- General database terms, the advantages of a relational database, and the basics of the Access interface and Access objects
- The fundamentals of good database design and normalization, and how to create and modify a database in Access and set keys and relationships
- How to create tables in design view, add fields in datasheet and design view, add validation rules for fields and tables, and better understand keys, indexes, and relationships
- How to create and modify basic queries and add calculated fields
- How to create simple forms, the basics of form design, and how to use form controls
- How to create reports and control data sources, how to add, move, and manipulate reports, and how to format reports and add images

This is the first course in a series. After you complete it, consider going on to the others:

- *Access 2016 Relational Database Management*

A note on class duration

The first two chapters of this course contain a lot of conceptual material, including a broad overview of Access and databases, and the basics of designing good relational databases. There are exercises to practice and discuss designing a database from the ground up. Class time could be considerably shorter if this material is modified or assigned outside of class. This might be useful if, for instance, students already know database concepts and design and only need information on using Access specifically.

Course setup

To complete this course, each student and instructor needs to have a computer running Access 2016. Setup instructions and activities are written assuming Windows 10; however, with slight modification the course works using Windows XP Service Pack 3, Windows Vista Service Pack 1, Windows 7, or Windows 8 or 8.1.

Hardware requirements for Windows 10 course setup include:

- 1 GHz or faster processor (32- or 64-bit) or SoC
- 1 GB (32-bit) or 2GB (64-bit) RAM
- 25 GB total hard drive space (50GB or more recommended)
- DirectX 9 (or later) video card or integrated graphics, with a minimum of 128 MB of graphics memory
- Monitor with 1280x800 or higher resolution
- Wi-Fi or Ethernet adapter
- Pads and pens or whiteboards and markers for collaborative database design

Software requirements include:

- Windows 10 (or alternative as above)
- Microsoft Access 2016 or any Microsoft Office 2016 32-bit edition that includes Access
- The Access 2016 Relational Database Design data files and PowerPoint slides, available at http://www.30bird.com

Note: It is a known issue that functions written in the 32-bit edition of Access might not run on the 64-bit edition of Access. This only applies to the version of Access/Office, not to Windows. The operating system can be 64-bit, but Access/Office must be 32-bit.

Network requirements include:

- An Internet connection in order to complete the exercise on downloading and using a template (which can be skipped or demonstrated by the instructor)

Because the exercises in this course include viewing and changing some Access defaults, it's recommended to begin with a fresh installation of the software. But this is certainly not necessary. Just be aware that if you are not using a fresh installation, some exercises might work slightly differently and some screens might look slightly different.

1. Install Windows 10, including all recommended updates and service packs. Use a different computer and user name for each student.
2. Install Microsoft Access 2016 (or Office 2016) 32-bit edition, using all defaults during installation.
3. Update Access or Office using Windows Update.
4. Copy the Access 2016 Relational Database Design data files to the Documents folder.

Chapter 1: Database fundamentals

You will learn:

- General database terms
- The advantages of a relational database
- How to navigate the Access interface
- The basics of Access objects

Module A: Understanding general database terms

Databases exist so that we can organize and easily access information. So, no matter which particular tool we're using to do that, there are some general terms you'll hear in any phase of designing, creating, querying or managing the database. We will explain the more common terms here, which should give you a solid foundation of knowledge about the basics. Knowing these terms not only will help you understand how Access applies them, but will allow you to transition into using other larger systems if you wish.

This module will give you an overview of:

- Database management systems
- Tables
- Queries and SQL

Database management systems

When is a database a DBMS?

A *database management system*, or *DBMS*, is software tool that can create a database and allow users to manage the data, commonly referred to as a database.

Technically, a software tool that we call a database is usually a Database Management System (or DBMS). Depending on the specific tool, we may be working with one database at a time like in Access, or many databases that are all part of one database server, like SQL Server or Oracle.

Consider that there are actually two main parts to Access, for example. There's the data we store, and the software that manages it. Given this internal separation, it should make sense to discover you could choose to use Access (the software) to manage data from SQL Server (or more precisely, its storage) if you'd like.

Normalization

Normalization is the process of organizing your data to reduce duplication and make sure the data is consistent. It is, in short, the right way to store data.

There are guidelines, of course, that help you store the data in the most efficient way possible, and one of the most important concepts to learn here is normalization. Database evangelists (people who are passionate about this sort of thing) like to talk about "normal forms," and the conversation can get pretty theoretical. Don't let it throw you.

Normalization in The Real World can be distilled down to a few practical concepts that are easy to apply. The idea when you're setting up data storage is to accomplish two major goals:

- Making it so that you do the minimum amount of work when you add new data or make changes
- Making it easy and efficient to get the data out when you need it

You will usually start work on normalizing a database during the design process, before you start storing any actual data. Ask any database evangelists about how hard it is to change your table design after the data is part of a living, breathing, being-used-every-day-by-real-people database. You'll understand why it's important to tackle this early.

Additionally, since normalization also has to do with making sure we have accurate, consistent data, you'll also want to make sure that once data is being stored, it's done the same way every time. For example: It's going to be much harder to find all your Pennsylvania customers are if the state is sometimes stored as "PA", other times as "Penn" and in still other cases using the full state name.

Referential integrity

Referential integrity helps make sure the information that links the smaller units of our data storage together are entered consistently, so that we can query ("ask the database a question") our information.

If you've used spreadsheets as a convenient way to store data, building your first database (Or trying to understand how an existing one is set up) can be a frustrating exercise. The reason for this is that we'll find data scattered all over the place into these storage units called tables, not all neat and lined up in one place like on a spreadsheet. However: Rejoice! This is actually one of the strengths of how databases manage information.

When we want to get our data back out though, to create that quarterly report, or to find out how many widgets our customers in the UK have bought in the last month, we're going to have to piece that data back together, from all those tables it lives in. In order make that work smoothly and accurately, we implement a concept called referential integrity.

Let's go with the example of our customers and their orders. The table that holds the information about my orders has hopefully quite a few records. Each record uniquely identifies my customer somehow, along with all the other information that's probably there about what they bought and how much it cost and how we shipped it. We could produce a report that prints out with that unique customer ID, but it's probably meaningless to The Boss. They want to see the company name, the name of the buyer at that company, etc., and that information is stored in a different table. When we correctly implement referential integrity between our tables, the process of getting that information into the report is a trivial exercise, and we'll know it's accurate.

Discussion: Access help

Let's use these following questions as a way to get you familiar with the extensive Help system in Access 2016. You can bring up the Help window by opening Access 2016 and clicking **?**. You might not fully understand the answers yet, but you will soon.

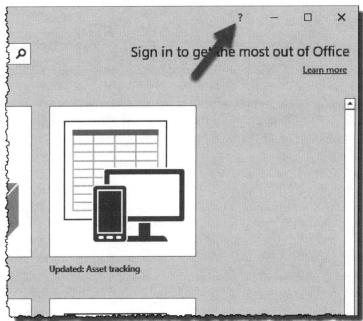

1. You create an Access database containing 3 tables. How many different files does Access use to store these 3 tables?

2. For normalization purposes, every row and column intersection should have a _____ value.

3. What is an "orphan" record and how does Access help you prevent this from happening in your database?

Table overview

Simply put, a *table* is a named container for data. Typically, a table is designed to contain specific types of data about one topic.

Tables in Access will be the hub around which all your other objects revolve. You use Forms to add new table data, change what's already in a table, or delete it. You use Queries to "ask the tables a question" about the data they contain. You use Reports to display table data in a formatted way. Tables will have a unique name in the database, along with a varying number of pieces of information. For example, a table storing data about your customers should probably include the company's name, its address and phone number(s), email addresses, etc.

Tables are also usually the container to which we assign permissions. For example: If we want certain users to be able to add and remove data, other users to only view the data, and to deny some other users access to the data altogether, we generally do that by allowing or denying these privileges at table level.

Part of your task in table design is to make sure that you're only storing information that's central to the topic in question. Our customers make orders, right? But we're not going to store the order information in the same table as the general customer information. We're probably going to create a separate table called (you guessed it) Orders, and leave a piece of data in the Orders table that tells us which customer made the order. This aspect of table design is part of normalization.

Fields

A *field* is an individual piece of data in a table that is created by assigning a name and a data type. Sometimes fields are referred to as columns. The field's *Data type* is a rule for what sort of information can be stored in the table field. A *Record* is one line item in a table, composed of values for the defined fields of that table. Records are also referred to as rows.

We can pretty easily draw the mental picture for you to have fields and records make sense. Maybe you already figured it out, since we sometimes we substitute the terms rows and columns. If we're storing our customers' invoice information, the table could potentially have fields that store the following:

- The customer's address as city, state and zip
- The date the order was placed
- The date the order was shipped
- How much they owe us
- What kind of discount they received, if any

In fact, if that data were stored in Excel, it might look something like this:

Ship Name	Ship Address	Ship City	Ship Region	Ship Postal Code	Order Date	Shipped Date	Extended Price	Discount
Island Trading	Garden House Crowther Way	Cowes	Isle of Wight	PO31 7PJ	13-Feb-16	23-Feb-16	$190.00	0.00%
Island Trading	Garden House Crowther Way	Cowes	Isle of Wight	PO31 7PJ	13-Feb-16	23-Feb-16	$800.00	0.00%
Island Trading	Garden House Crowther Way	Cowes	Isle of Wight	PO31 7PJ	13-Feb-16	23-Feb-16	$60.00	0.00%
Island Trading	Garden House Crowther Way	Cowes	Isle of Wight	PO31 7PJ	13-Feb-16	23-Feb-16	$714.00	0.00%
Reggiani Caseifici	Strada Provinciale 124	Reggio Emilia		42100	02-Feb-16	12-Feb-16	$180.00	10.00%
Reggiani Caseifici	Strada Provinciale 124	Reggio Emilia		42100	02-Feb-16	12-Feb-16	$1,252.80	10.00%
Reggiani Caseifici	Strada Provinciale 124	Reggio Emilia		42100	02-Feb-16	12-Feb-16	$260.00	0.00%
Ricardo Adocicados	Av. Copacabana, 267	Rio de Janeiro	RJ	02389-890	05-Feb-16	09-Feb-16	$182.40	20.00%
Ricardo Adocicados	Av. Copacabana, 267	Rio de Janeiro	RJ	02389-890	05-Feb-16	09-Feb-16	$420.00	0.00%
QUICK-Stop	Taucherstraße 10	Cunewalde		01307	06-Jun-15	07-Jun-15	$990.00	10.00%
QUICK-Stop	Taucherstraße 10	Cunewalde		01307	06-Jun-15	07-Jun-15	$513.00	10.00%
Split Rail Beer & Ale	P.O. Box 555	Lander	WY	82520	08-Feb-16	15-Feb-16	$360.00	0.00%
Split Rail Beer & Ale	P.O. Box 555	Lander	WY	82520	08-Feb-16	15-Feb-16	$318.00	0.00%
Lehmanns Marktstand	Magazinweg 7	Frankfurt a.M.		60528	31-May-15	06-Jun-15	$576.00	20.00%
Lehmanns Marktstand	Magazinweg 7	Frankfurt a.M.		60528	31-May-15	06-Jun-15	$960.00	0.00%
Lehmanns Marktstand	Magazinweg 7	Frankfurt a.M.		60528	31-May-15	06-Jun-15	$414.24	20.00%
Lehmanns Marktstand	Magazinweg 7	Frankfurt a.M.		60528	31-May-15	06-Jun-15	$368.00	20.00%
Folk och fä HB	Åkergatan 24	Bräcke		S-844 67	09-Feb-16	01-Mar-16	$115.80	0.00%
Folk och fä HB	Åkergatan 24	Bräcke		S-844 67	09-Feb-16	01-Mar-16	$135.00	0.00%
Drachenblut Delikatessen	Walserweg 21	Aachen		52066	09-Feb-16	14-Feb-16	$374.76	0.00%
Drachenblut Delikatessen	Walserweg 21	Aachen		52066	09-Feb-16	14-Feb-16	$656.00	0.00%
La maison d'Asie	1 rue Alsace-Lorraine	Toulouse		31000	10-May-15	18-May-15	$176.70	5.00%
La maison d'Asie	1 rue Alsace-Lorraine	Toulouse		31000	10-May-15	18-May-15	$346.56	5.00%
Rancho grande	Av. del Libertador 900	Buenos Aires		1010	13-Feb-16	06-Mar-16	$405.00	0.00%

The process of normalization will more than likely lead us to storing this data in two or more separate tables to avoid duplication like you see here, but you get the idea. Since each order is a unique "event," think of a field as an individual piece of information that becomes part of a record.

Data types

Since we're also concerned with consistency, each named field will also have a *data type*, which is generally what kind of information the data is. We don't want our order date to store the value "yesterday", right? We need a real calendar date, and if we assign the right data type to that field, we restrict the value that can be stored. In a field that's set to "Date/Time" in Access 2016, entering "yesterday" will be rejected, but entering "April 17, 2022" will be accepted.

Though the specifics vary from one DBMS to the next, there are really just a few broad categories of data types: Text, number, date/time, true/false, then other special use types. Many data types will also require you to further specify constraints for that type. For example:

- If you're allowing someone to enter their name in a field, how many characters can the longest name be? (Or how few can the shortest one be, for that matter)
- If you're storing numbers, what kind of number: Whole numbers? Fixed point decimals that represent money? Or "floating point" numbers that have more meaning for percentages or math operations?
- If you're storing date information, are we also storing the time of day along with it?

When you design a table in Access, you will choose the data type for each field from a list.

Special use types will vary widely based on the capabilities of each database. Some of the more interesting data types that Access 2016 supports for table fields include

- *AutoNumber*: Automatically assigns a numeric value to the field in new records, by adding some specific amount to the last allocated value.
- *Hyperlink*: Allows display of text that displays like the links on a web page, and when clicked takes the user to an existing field, web page, or email client.
- *Attachment*: Stores references to potentially multiple fields in one field, and lets the user open the attachment in its native program (So if you store a PDF document in an attachment field, you can open it in your PDF reader directly from Access)

Table metadata

In general, the term *metadata* refers to data about the data. With a picture file, for instance, information about the picture - such as subject matter and camera settings - can be stores along with the picture. This is metadata.

Metadata for Access tables helps with the storage, organization, and retrieval of data. Here are four important types of table metadata:

Indexes　　A separate set of storage the database maintains that allows it to find information in the fastest way possible. Indexes are created at table level. Each table can have multiple indexes, each of which could contain multiple fields.

Primary Key(s)　　The field or fields that uniquely identify a record.

Foreign Key(s)　　The field or fields that links back to more information in a related table.

Relationships　　A link between two tables that specifies the type of association between the primary key field on one table and the foreign key field of another.

Indexes

Consider the way you might find a specific piece of information about what's in a reference book. The least efficient way would be to read the entire book from front to back, and note the locations of where your word or phrase occurred. In a table without indexes though, this is roughly what a database's query engine has to do: Scan the table record by record, and see if the information in each record matches what the user is looking for.

We help the database be more efficient with an index. What is it you do in Real Life when you're looking for a specific word or phrase in a book? You use the index! Worth noting, it's a separate set of pages that lists topics, key words, concepts, phrases in alphabetical order along with a page number. Want to know where they mention normalization in a database book? Check the index, find the page number, and there you go.

When we design tables, we add one or more indexes. Then each time someone adds a new record or changes an existing one, the database doesn't just update the record itself—it updates that separate storage area called the index, too. That way, the next time a user looks for data, the database engine uses the index to find the exact record(s) it needs quickly, even if those records are scattered throughout different locations in its internal storage.

If this sounds complicated, don't worry! Access 2016 and other databases have internal formulas that choose from the available indexes, and pick the fastest way to get you your data. Your only job is to make sure that indexes exist for the fields you're going to ask for most often.

Key fields

The more you learn about querying a database, the more you'll see how the concept of indexes and key fields are tied together, because we're typically writing queries that includes these key fields as the values we join two tables together with. A *primary key* is a field or fields (Though multi-field primary keys are rare in Access) that uniquely identifies a record. For our customer example, it could be their unique customer number.

In most databases, if there isn't a naturally occurring unique value, we create one. That's typically the purpose of giving a field the AutoNumber data type in Access. Then we just use that automatically assigned number as the unique identifier for the record everywhere else we need to in the database. When we do that, the value is called a *foreign key*, in that it refers back to a primary key value in some other table. Following a customers and orders example, the Customer ID field in the customers table would be our primary key, while the Customer ID that shows up in each order record would be called the foreign key. Typically, we use the exact same name for matching sets of primary and foreign key fields, but it's not required.

Relationships

As we build our database, we as humans certainly understand that our data is related. But since we're human, we also know that we need rules to make sure that the data stays consistent. After all, what if someone tries to enter an ID for a customer who doesn't exist? That's where relationships come in: We formalize the association between the table with the primary key and the one with the foreign key.

When we create a relationship, we create an association. You can decide on what rules the association puts on the table values. If each customer can have many orders (And let's hope they do!) the relationship will be called One-to-Many. If we had a table that stored records about a customer's credit line, Access would make that a One-to-One relationship, if for each customer there was exactly one credit line.

The configurable part for you is that you can decide what happens when the "one" side of the relationship (The primary key value) changes or is deleted. The options range from just plain not allowing a change or deletion in the primary key field, to cascading that change to all the related tables' foreign key fields or records.

Discussion: Metadata

1. You've imported data from another source into Access 2016, but you're not sure the tables are normalized. What tool does Access provide to help you figure that out?

2. How can I see all the existing relationships between tables in my database?

3. You have a table that needs a primary key, and you identify a field named LastOrderDate that automatically updates every time a customer makes a new order. Why is this a bad choice for a possible primary key field?

Queries and SQL

When we want to get information from our database, we write a query. A query is just a "question" we ask the database: We're asking to see records, update values in existing records, create new tables, give permissions... and so much more! That query is created in *SQL*, or *Structured Query Language*, and often pronounced "Sequel." SQL has the advantage of having been around since the 1970s, so you'll find plenty of documentation about how to create these queries. SQL syntax, since it's "mature," works across varied database platforms. SQL language references may mention something called *ANSI-standard SQL*, which means the code should work in any database that supports the SQL language. While the standard is maintained by the American National Standards Institute, each vendor is free to add their own syntax that usually only works on their platform. Microsoft SQL Server, for example, uses a version call Transact-SQL, or T-SQL for short.

The good news is that Access 2016 hides the complexity of much of the heavy lifting SQL does for us. When you're looking at the Datasheet view of a Table, for instance, Access has executed a SELECT query on our behalf. But it's good to know at least some little bits of SQL, though, in case you need to customize things, especially for queries and reports.

SQL statements can be split into several broad categories: DDL, DCL and DML. In actual practice, it's not necessary to know what your query is—You'll simply write it using the statements that do what you need to get done. Academically though, the divisions do exist. *DDL* (Data Definition Language) statements would begin with SQL keywords like *CREATE, ALTER* or *DROP*. DML (Data Manipulation Language) statements do the "CRUD" work, a common abbreviation for "Create, Retrieve, Update, Delete". These statements begin with *SELECT, INSERT, UPDATE* or *DELETE*. Finally, DCL (Data Control Language) statements allow or deny users the ability to perform certain database tasks. These statements start with the keywords *Grant, Deny* or *Revoke*.

SQL statements

A query is a SQL statement that performs a database task. Seems like a pretty simple definition, right? Well, it is. Any interaction we have with our data, from creating the database itself, to changing the fields in a table, to adding, selecting or deleting data, to allowing a new group of users to access a table, is done with a query.

Consider the example of a database that contains information about our customers and their orders. If we wanted to see all the data in all the customer fields, we could execute a SQL query like this in a query editor, a tool that connects to our database:

```
SELECT * FROM CustomersTable
```

(While it's almost never necessary to capitalize SQL keywords, this is a standard syntax convention for many SQL programmers and applications, to distinguish the language keywords from our own syntax).

If we only wanted to see certain fields, we substitute a comma-separated list of those fields in place of the asterisk (*) in the previous statement:

```
SELECT ID, Customer_Name, Customer_Contact FROM CustomersTable
```

When we only request a subset of the fields in a table, we call that vertical filtering of the results (Think of the table data like a spreadsheet, with the column names across the top). Just to take the example one step further, we can also do horizontal filtering by restricting which records we return:

```
SELECT ID, Customer_Name, Customer_Contact FROM CustomersTable WHERE Customer_Status='ACTIVE'
```

These are some basic examples, just to show a progression from a very simply query to something that has a bit more "flash." SQL provides quite a few ways to take queries you've written and re-use them, too. For example, if you'd like to see just certain columns and certain rows from a table or tables, you can save that as a View object, and users can query it just like a table. If you'd like to be able to pass in different data values every time you run the query, or group multiple statements together as one unit, you can create a Stored Procedure.

(A word of caution: Not every database implements this the same way. Perhaps confusingly in Access, for example, what we defined above as a View shows up in the Queries tab.)

Exercise: Exploring a query

Access 2016 uses the SQL language without our having to write the code ourselves. Let's look at a query, make some changes, and notice how the SQL query Access is using changes.

Do This	How & Why
1. Click **Start > Access 2016**	To open Access.
2. Click **Updated: Contacts**	You'll create a new database from this template.
3. Change the name to `ContactsDemo.accdb` and then click **Create**.	The new database opens. Several objects have already been created.
4. In the yellow Security Warning bar, click Enable Content.	If necessary. Whether or not you see this depends on your security settings.
5. Close the introduction screen.	
6. In the Navigation Pane on the left, under the Queries section, double-click the **Contacts Extended** query.	You'll examine the SQL behind this view.
7. On the Home tab of the ribbon, click the **View** button.	(Don't click the drop-down arrow.) You see the design view of the query. The is the graphical way to create a query.
8. Click the **View** drop-down arrow and select **SQL View**.	Notice the complexity of the language following the SELECT keyword at the beginning of the statement.
9. From the View drop-down list, select **Design View**.	You'll edit the query.
10. Select the first two columns in the bottom pane and click **Delete Columns** (or press **Delete**).	**Delete Columns** To select columns, click at the very top of the column. Hold **Shift** to select multiple columns. Deleting them will remove them from the query statement.
11. Switch back to SQL View and examine the SQL statement.	It has been dramatically simplified.
12. Click **File > Save As > Save Object As**, and then click the **Save As** button.	
13. Edit the name to read `Simple Contacts Query` and then click **OK**.	
14. Click **File > Close**.	To close the database.

Assessment: Database terms

1. What reduces redundant data?

    - Normalization
    - Referential Integrity
    - Metadata
    - Indexing

2. Which is a field or fields that link back to more information in a related table.

    - Primary key
    - Related key
    - Foreign key
    - Index Key

Module B: Relational databases

In a relational database, data is usually organized into multiple tables, each holding a specific type of data. The tables are related to each other with key fields, allowing data to be accessed and reorganized quickly without having to reorganize the actual tables. We'll compare these to other types of databases.

You will learn about:

- Flat file databases
- NoSQL databases
- Relational databases

Flat file databases

A *flat file database* store all its data in one table. If you've worked with Microsoft Excel, Lotus Notes or Google Sheets, you know about the data storage capabilities of spreadsheets. These applications feature the ability to create formulas that refer to other cells and perform calculations on the data. The features can be fairly sophisticated, and often lead to power users referring to their application as "my Excel database." If we're defining a database as simply somewhere to store data, then obviously these sorts of applications qualify.

NoSQL databases

Another style of data storage that's gained popularity in recent years is called a NoSQL database. Created to deal with modern applications that scale over the web (Think mobile devices and their data), NoSQL databases don't have the same stringent rules that, say, SQL Server and Access have. In database terms, those rules are called a *schema*, so you'll hear NoSQL databases referred to as *schema-free storage*. While NoSQL databases still organize data into structures called tables, each record could have an almost completely different set of fields. For example, if one customer had 3 phone numbers, we might choose to store them all in one record in a NoSQL table. In a relational database with its rules about normalization, this would be considered poor design.

Advantages of relational databases

Each database type can be the best solution for a given need, depending on the way you need to store and retrieve the data, and the experience level of the people doing it. For people who haven't used Access and don't understand relationships, for example, seeing everything all in one place in an application like Excel can make it easier for them to work with their data, since there's no work required other than entering the data into a single, easy-to-read spreadsheet.

A relational database is the data storage method we use when we're breaking up our data into smaller storage units (tables) and we need to maintain referential integrity. This gives us consistency: The same types of data stored in the same way, by definition. In fact, we expect with relational databases that we'll be storing the same types of information about each record. Our customer table example might have fields for the customer's name, address, phone number, etc. Let's assume we have different people we talk to at the company. In a relational database, that might lead us to create another table (Let's say we call it CustomerContacts), where each record in CustomerContacts includes the unique id of the customer from the original main Customers table.

Imagine now that the name of the customer's company changes. In a flat file database, we'd have to potentially make that change in multiple locations. When we store data about customer orders in a spreadsheet, each line that contained the order information would also have the customer information. We might be doing a lot of maintenance of our data, with the inherent risk of mistyping it somewhere or not finding all the places we need to do the update. In a relational database, we simply make the change in one place (The original main Customers table) and then display that result when we do a query by joining the appropriate tables.

As we said, there *are* valid business reasons for using any of the database types we've mentioned. With Access 2016, you're automatically reaping the benefit of relational data storage:

- Records stored in tables that are governed by a set schema that you design.
- Easy updating of existing data since each unique record only exists in one row of one table.
- SQL queries that bring the smaller units (tables) together to display them as one unit for reporting purposes.

Exercise: Importing a flat file

Access can import data from other types of databases. In this exercise, we'll import data from an Excel worksheet into a new table in our Access database.

Do This	How & Why
1. Open `ContactsDemo`.	You'll import data from an Excel spreadsheet into an Access table.
2. On the External Data ribbon tab, click **Excel**.	
3. Click **Browse** and navigate to the current module folder.	
4. Select `Excel Orders.xlsx` and then click **Open**.	Be sure the first option is selected - to import the source data into a new table.
5. Click **OK**.	
6. Click **Next**.	Leave the box checked, because the file has a header row.
7. Click **Next**.	
8. Select **Choose my own primary key**.	It will select the first field - OrderID.
9. Click **Next**.	You'll leave the default name as is.
10. Click **Finish** and then click **Close**.	You won't save the settings. A new tables appear in the navigation pane named Orders.

Assessment: Relational Databases

1. An Excel spreadsheet is what kind of database?

   - Relational
   - NoSQL
   - Flat file
   - It's not a database

2. Which database type was developed for use over the web?

   - NoSQL
   - SQL
   - WebDB
   - Flat file

Module C: Access interface and objects

You can find the Access 2016 application on your Start menu. If you open it this way, you'll see a screen where you choose to open an existing database or create a new one. The last few databases you've opened will display on the Recent tab on the left side of the window. Keep in mind that if you've moved the file to a different folder since the last time you had Access open, the application won't automatically find the file in its new location.

You will learn about:

- The Access interface
- Access objects

New databases

If you want to start completely from scratch, with just a blank slate and objects created for you, just click the Blank Database tile when you get to the Access opening view. This is what you see when you open Access from the Start Menu. You'll see similar options when you click the File tab and then click **New**.

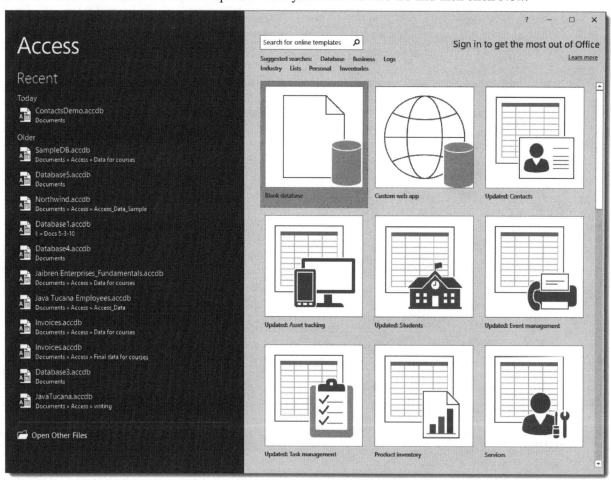

You might notice a link in the box where you're naming your new database that says "Should I create an Access app or a desktop database?" We're dealing here exclusively with what is referred to here as a desktop database: A stand-alone Access database that contains all its own data. An "Access app" is used when you want to use the Access interface elements (Forms, Reports, etc.) to manage data that's stored in either an Office 365 or SharePoint database, so you'd have to provide a valid URL to link to that data.

You might want to also take a few moments to browse through a wide array of template databases available here for common use cases, everything from event management to contacts, product inventory, or students in a school. (As you scroll down the list, notice some of the templates are labeled as SharePoint web apps, the kind we just talked about). You don't have to use the templates exactly "as is," but it's a good starting point if you're not sure about how to build your own from the ground up. Just because it's a template doesn't mean you can't make changes to it later.

You can also search for templates online from the search box on top if you don't find one that fits your needs.

Existing databases

You can open existing databases from the File tab, or directly from the Explorer window—Just look for that .ACCDB file wherever you saved it and double-click it. If you open it this way, you'll skip directly to the Home tab of your database, where you'll see all the objects displayed that are already part of your .ACCDB file.

For users of older versions of Access, you should know that the file format used by Access changed as of the 2007 version. If you have a database saved in the old format known as Access 97, Microsoft recommends that you use the older version of Access to open the file and convert it to the new .ACCDB format (Details on the exact steps to do this are available here from Microsoft Support: https://support.microsoft.com/en-us/kb/2755119)

The navigation pane

The Navigation Pane along the left side of Access is your quick and easy way to see whatever you want in your database.

If you create a new blank database, Access will just display a Tables tab with the sample Table1 table, waiting for you to add fields (You can always delete this table if you want). Click the drop-down arrow in the Navigation Pane to see other views of the database. You can create custom groups of objects, typically for a set of items all related to one task, like a table to store the data, a query to select it, and a form to manipulate it might all go together in one custom group if you want.

Right-click in the Navigation Pane and choose Navigation Options to change the display to your liking. Commonly used options are

- Choosing to make Hidden Objects visible or not. Sometimes we have tables that are around to provide options for drop-down boxes in forms, for example (We call them Lookup Tables), but maybe we don't need our users to see them and be distracted from their main data mission.

- Filtering the Object Types that show up as an option. Maybe we choose to hide the Macros and Modules displays if we don't want anyone to have an easy way to see (and maybe change) our code.

- Allowing objects to be opened with a single- or double-click.

Exercise: Using the navigation pane

The Navigation Pane is the nerve center of your Access database. It allows you to see all the objects you've created, manage those views and create custom groups of objects for easy viewing. In this exercise, we will use the Navigation Pane options to make navigating our database easier.

Do This	How & Why
1. Open the `ContactsDemo` database from its saved location, if necessary. 2. Click the drop-down arrow at the top right of the Navigation Pane and click **Tables and Related Views**	
3. Click the same drop-down arrow and choose **All Access Objects**.	To restore the original view.
4. Right-click in the Navigation Pane and click **Navigation Options**, and then in the category list click **Object Type**.	
5. Clear the check boxes next to **Macros** and **Modules** to hide these object categories from the Navigation Pane view.	
6. Click **OK**.	

Access objects

The term object is used often in computer science, programming, and applications. In Access and other databases, objects are the things you usually see in the navigation pane. The objects you'll deal with most to start are tables, queries, forms, and reports. More advanced objects include macros and code modules.

Tables

Everything else you do in Access 2016 depends on your tables. These are the storage units that we'll work with to get data from in Queries, to show and/or change in Forms, and to display in Reports. From the Home tab in Access, Tables are displayed by default in the Navigation Pane window along the left side of the screen.

If you want to get to know how these objects operate, you might want to create a new database from one of those templates we mentioned earlier (The one labeled Students should give you a pretty interesting variety of objects). Every template will create many objects, and there will always be some tables included. If you use spreadsheets, use the Datasheet view of the table to see a very familiar looking screen. To see more about the specifics of each field, switch to Design view.

Queries

A query is a question we ask the database. You can think of the Queries tab in the Navigation Pane window as listing all the questions we've saved and given names to. We can ask these questions over and over any time we want.

The most common type of query by far is one that selects existing data. If you've got that Students database sample for example, everything in the Queries tab is a Select query. You can double-click any of them to see the Datasheet view of the results (Though there won't be any data if you haven't done anything else with the template yet). If you'd like to see the SQL syntax that's actually running, choose SQL VIEW from the Views button on the ribbon when you've got a query selected. If you change any of the SQL code, you are changing what the query does.

Forms

Forms are the more elegant way we manipulate data from tables or queries. This user-friendly format puts some pretty robust functionality into the user experience over the simple (and sometimes intimidating) Datasheet view from the Tables section, such as:

- Buttons you can link to Macros or other event-handling code. Want to add the current records to your contacts in Outlook? There's a macro for that (The Guardian Details form in our sample database has one of those)

- Controls to give the user a set of choices in a list box or a drop-down box, ideal for restricting data entry to a small set of allowable values you decide on.

- A display that incorporates both the Datasheet view and a Form view called a Split form to give the users the best of both worlds!

Take a look at the Forms section of the Navigation Pane window for more examples. Bound forms, which is to say a form that has controls that are tied to a certain set of data, can be created easily using the Form Wizard from the Create tab on the ribbon as a starting point.

Reports

Access 2016 reports are the way we display data with the purpose of seeing a summary or doing calculations on groups of records. Reports look good right there on the screen, and they're meant to be printed.

Creation of Access reports forces you to think a little differently than you do with the Datasheet view of a table or the standard view of a Form. In those instances, we're dealing with one record at a time. We create Reports based on using the provided sections, so we would design a header and a footer for the whole page or the whole report for example. But then we have the option of creating placeholders for each record, and then have Access fill those placeholders with however much data we ask for from the table or query. So, you design the placeholders for the record once, and then Access will fill it—With one record, 100 records, 1000 records, and so on.

Additionally, you can create groups of records and do a summary of group-related data. If the report shows each of our customer's order as one record, we could also create group sections that total up how much they've spent, either overall or by some subset of the records that we decide on, like each month, each year, etc.

We can also choose the sort the output of a report in any way we want, unrelated to the actual order of the records in the table or query.

Exercise: Examining objects

In this exercise, we'll get a quick look at how Access objects are related. Typically, we create a table to store the data, a query to give ourselves a different view of the data, a form to edit it and a report to display or print it out.

Do This	How & Why
1. Open `ContactsDemo`.	
2. In the Navigation pane, click the drop-down arrow at the top and click **Tables and Related Views**.	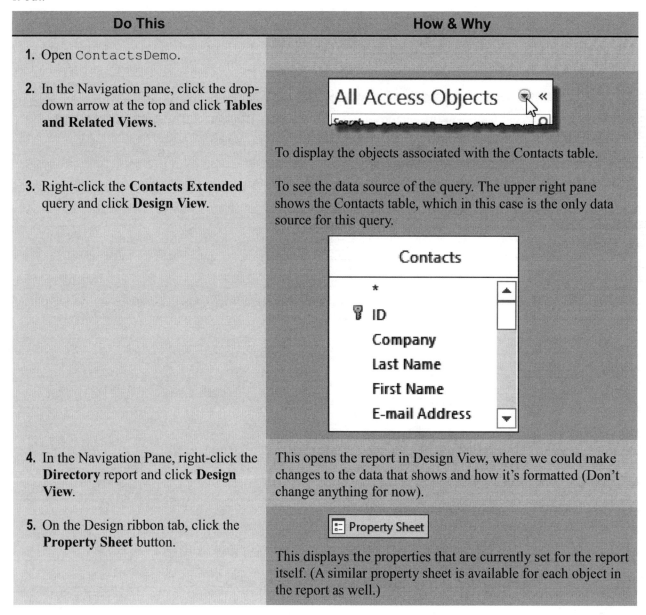 To display the objects associated with the Contacts table.
3. Right-click the **Contacts Extended** query and click **Design View**.	To see the data source of the query. The upper right pane shows the Contacts table, which in this case is the only data source for this query.
4. In the Navigation Pane, right-click the **Directory** report and click **Design View**.	This opens the report in Design View, where we could make changes to the data that shows and how it's formatted (Don't change anything for now).
5. On the Design ribbon tab, click the **Property Sheet** button.	This displays the properties that are currently set for the report itself. (A similar property sheet is available for each object in the report as well.)

Do This	How & Why
6. In the property sheet, next to Record Source, click as shown.	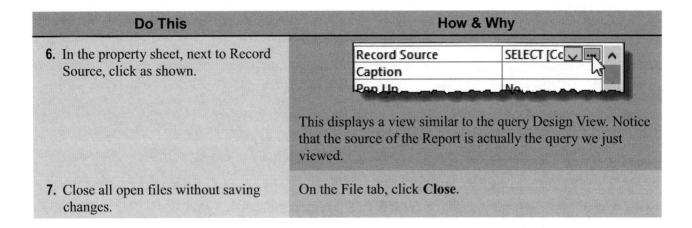 This displays a view similar to the query Design View. Notice that the source of the Report is actually the query we just viewed.
7. Close all open files without saving changes.	On the File tab, click **Close**.

Assessment: Access interface and objects

1. What is the file extension for an Access database?

   - .mdbx
   - .accdx
   - .accdb
   - .xlsx

2. Which is used for easier on-screen input of data?

   - Form
   - Table
   - Report
   - Query

Summary: Database fundamentals

In this chapter, we explored the general underpinnings of relational databases. We got our first look at how Access works to implement the features that relational databases support, and we dove into the Access 2016 interface to see how we could work with existing databases by using the Navigation Pane.

You now know how to:

- Define what a relational database is and what features it offers vs. a flat-file or No-SQL database
- Open Access 2016
- Open an existing database or create a new one from a template
- Change the Navigation pane view to show or hide groups of objects

Synthesis: Discussing database fundamentals

Your growing company has been using Excel spreadsheets for most of its data storage. This is becoming cumbersome as data entry errors increase due to more frequent updating, and management demands more sophisticated reporting.

1. What reasons could you give for moving the existing data to a relational database?

2. What reasons could you give for moving the existing data to an Access 2016 database?

Chapter 2: Database design

You will learn:

- The fundamentals of good database design
- About database normalization
- How to create and modify a database
- About keys and relationships

Module A: Fundamentals of efficient design

Before diving into the Access 2016 application, we'll take a step back and see how all the pieces are going to fit together before we create anything. The process starts with - and largely depends on - an efficient table design, and we'll spend the bulk of this chapter on doing just that, along with the key fields and relationships that tie the tables together so we can run queries that work well later.

You will learn about:

- The goals of good design
- Modeling and model types

The goals of design

Why is it important to design before we create the database? Because otherwise, as we add more and more data to our tables, we'll find that our queries run slower, and in the case of Access 2016, just bogs down the whole interface. Not a good deal, but you can make sure your database works well right from the start *and* as you add data. That's one of the ways you know you're doing it right: Your database functions just as efficiently with 1,000,000 records as it did with 100 records.

The goals of design are to have a database that...

- *Gets data quickly.* This is probably the *single most important reason* for creating normalized tables, key fields, and indexes. Generally, the vast majority of all query activity in *any* database is for data selection (As opposed to inserts, updates, deletes or other specific types of queries).

- *Does inserts, updates and deletes quickly.* Internally, databases lock some records in a table during these operations. The quicker we get it done, the quicker these locks are released so that users have access to not only the updated or new records, but other records that may have been locked during that process.

- *Can have its schema updated with a minimum of effort.* Changes happen, inevitably. If we've tied ourselves into knots with our table design, we're going to have to untie (and re-tie?) the knots if we want to change our table structure. Normalized tables go a long way toward implementing this requirement.

This is an important, time-consuming task, and it's basically up to you, with no initial help from any sort of wizard in an application. (Access does have a Table Analyzer tool, but it's not something you should rely on in lieu of a well-thought out table design, and it only works to analyze existing tables). This is work we do before we ever create the first field in the first table. There are software patterns that advocate developing these models in stages rather than all at once, and that's fine. The important thing is to know what tables your field are going into—and why they're going there—before you add the first record.

Discussion: Database design basics

Let's answer the following questions using the extensive Help system in Access 2016. You can bring up the Help window by opening the Access 2016 application and clicking the **?** icon

1. Why is it important to understand the database design process before creating tables?

2. Why are relationships between tables important to efficient database design?

3. How does creating tables with the correct fields make it more likely you'll have accurate data?

Modeling

Let's think of our database conceptually first. Once we have a conceptual design for the database, we'll refine that into a logical design, and then into a physical design (Which—finally—will be our Access 2016 tables and fields).

In the software development world, when we don't have any code written yet, we depend on stories. Formally, they're called Use Cases or User Scenarios depending what methodology you use. Ultimately, they're just descriptions of what needs to be done with our eventual software, who's doing it, and how.

Here's an informal sample: "Logged-On User adds Product(s) to Shopping Cart. Shopping Cart items are purchased using Payment, and Logged-On User receives notification of success and order receipt." That's pretty straightforward, and it's only one of many stories. There are others for what happens when the user's not logged in, when their payment method fails, when they leave without buying what's in their shopping cart, and on and on.

The point is, we look at those stories and start to identify the type(s) of data we're going to need to store in the database to make this happen. Put all those stories together and you start to get an idea of what tables you'll be creating and what general sorts of information they'll have. We keep it general at this point.

The conceptual model

The end result of the conceptual design phase is usually an ERD, short for Entity Relationship Diagram. The "big picture" objects that eventually become one or more tables are called Entities, and we draw a general idea of how they'll be related. We know Customers are going to be related to Orders somehow, but again, the exact implementation details don't matter at this level. In fact, at this phase, the goal isn't even related to the eventual database design. We just want to identify, from a business needs perspective, what the major parts of our application are, and an ERD gets us going on that path.

The model we'll produce here should identify two things:

- Entities
- Relationships

There are a variety of modeling tools available out there, but if you want, it's perfectly acceptable just to sketch it out freehand. The important thing at this point is to understand the Big Picture of your database and the major subjects (We'll call them Entities) that your database is going to use. For example, this could be an initial ERD of our fictional customers database:

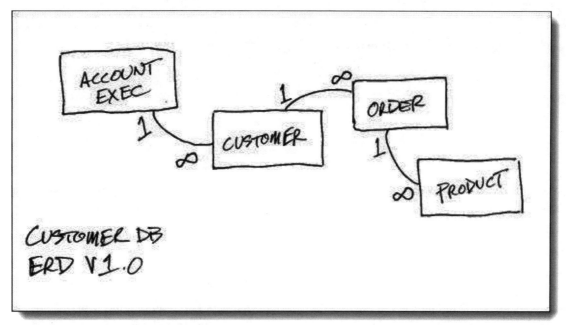

It looks simple, but it identifies that every Account Executive could have multiple Customers, every Customer could have multiple Orders, and every Order could have multiple Products. If this concept makes sense, then the rest of this step should, too, because all we're doing from here is identifying more entities and more relationships between the entities.

Exercise: Creating a conceptual design

Consider the information given to you by the Analyst team, in preparation for creating a new database for a medical office. Identify the entities, and the relationships between them, and draw an ERD to represent this conceptual database model. Don't get bogged down in details yet; you can start to drill down in the next phase.

> **State Analysis for Medical Office Database**
>
> This office consists of a variable number of medical providers, some doctors and some medical assistants. The office sees patients daily for both pre-set appointment times and walk-ins. Walk-ins are screened by a medical assistant, and then either referred to an in-house doctor or to an outside provider if possible. Medical assistants are not assigned billing responsibility.
>
> Patients typically have more than one doctor in this office, and sometimes see multiple doctors during one visit. Each doctor/patient interaction is billed separately and recorded as a separate appointment, even though they may occur back-to-back.
>
> The office generates bills for patients and insurance providers, but the client has requested that our database simply tracks payment amounts received and not whether they are from insurance or self-paid by the patient. The client will be maintaining a separate billing software. For convenience, our database should store patients addresses and note whether the address is their home and/or is for billing.

Do This	How & Why
1. Look for nouns in the User Story above. As you start to write them down, figure out how they might group together. Identify the entities.	Think about how and why the particular noun exists. If a patient has an address, for example, consider that we don't care about the address unless it's tied to a patient. So, in this case, address is more likely going to end up being a field(s) in a table rather than a table itself. Patient is an entity. Address probably not.
2. Draw all the entities you've identified on a piece of paper, with the name of the entity inside a rectangle.	
3. Consider if 2 entities are related. If so, draw a line between them and indicate the kind of relationship.	You can use symbols (Like 1 and the infinity symbol for 1-to-many), or a few words that describe the relationships (For example, you might write "has many" above the line for a 1-to-many relationship).
4. Look at your finished ERD. Does it accurately describe the major subjects of the database you've been charged with creating? Are there any entities you've missed? Any that should be eliminated?	Remember to not take on extra work, or make assumptions about anything that isn't specified in the User Story you read)

A sample of the finished ERD from the above story might look something like this. Answers may vary. Have students justify their reasons for the entities and relationships.

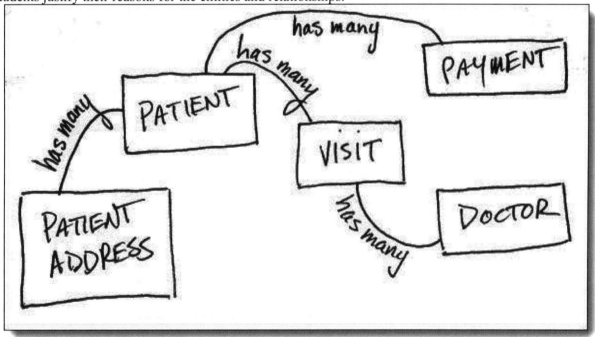

The logical model

Think of the logical model as the first place we start to think about the details of our data. If we have an entity called Customers from the ERD, we can start to identify what it is about a Customer that we will want to have as part of the eventual tables and their records. What's important here is creating another level of detail that takes us from the high-level concept of the ERD to something that looks more like our table structure will eventually.

Since we're not a physical design level yet, you'll still see some abstractions. Knowing that a customer needs to have his address saved in the database is more important than splitting it up into street, city, state, and zip. You do that in the physical design phase. Also, since the ERD has relationships built in already, this would be the level where we would start identifying where primary key and foreign key fields go, again without necessarily having to give them the field names they'll have later. It's enough to know that they logically belong in a certain place. The model we'll produce here will expand on the Conceptual model and add:

- Attributes
- Keys (Primary & Foreign)

One thing we shouldn't worry about from the conceptual level is how to implement many-to-many relationships. For now, it's enough to know that the relationship between the entities exists. We'll flesh this out once we physically create the tables.

We can continue with our example of a database for customers and their orders. With the help of User Stories, what we already know about our industry, other resources, etc., we can start to identify the attributes each entity has. We might move to a more formal modeling tool here, but if you wanted to keep sketching, you could. We continue with the Customers database model here, and we've listed some attributes for our entities:

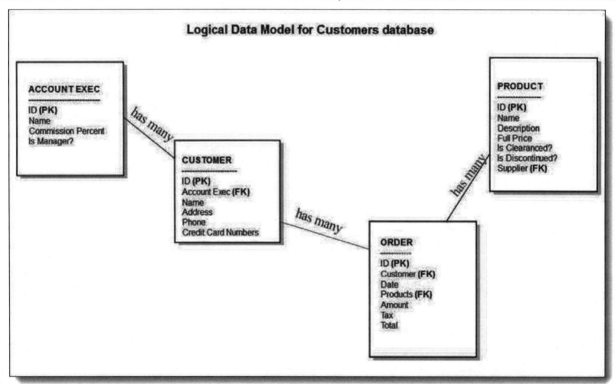

Notice what's been added. We've identified the attributes each entity has and what the key information should be. Primary key attributes are designated with a (PK) after the attribute, foreign keys with (FK).

Some of these attributes will end up being fields as-is. In the Account Exec entity, the attributes ID, Commission Percent and Is Manager could end up being fields just the way they are. In the Customer entity, expect that Name will probably become at least two fields, for first name and last name. Address will end up being split into street address, city, state and zip.

Note also that our design process has identified other entities. This is a common occurrence when modeling, and usually results in creating another version of the model to incorporate the new entities or attributes. In the model above, notice that the Product entity has a Supplier attribute, identified as a foreign key. The Customer entity has a Credit Card Numbers attribute, which will end up being stored in a separate table for normalization purposes. So, we might refine the model right here in the logical phase to look like this.

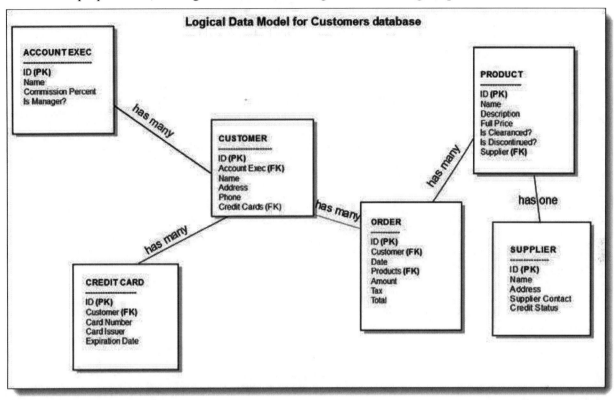

Exercise: Creating a logical design

Continue using the medical database example from the previous exercise, and create a logical data model from the conceptual one we did earlier. Here's what our conceptual model should look like so far.

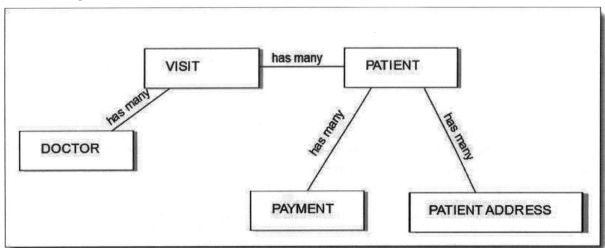

Do This	How & Why
1. Using your knowledge of the user stories (And in this case, general knowledge about how medical offices work), identify attributes for each entity and add them to the model.	Keep it general. It's not necessary to define the parts of an address yet.
2. Consider the relationships between the entities and add (PK) or (FK) to the attributes that will relate two tables together.	Not all attributes will be primary or foreign keys. You should have a primary key for each entity. Whether or not you have a foreign key will depend on the type of relationship the entity has to other entities.
3. Are there any attributes that should be entities on their own?	Look for places where an attribute could indicate that we'd have to store multiple facts in one attribute. For example, if a patient could have zero, one, or two phone numbers, we might have to change our eventual table design, and account for that here in the logical phase.
4. Look at your finished logical model. Does it still accurately reflect the relationships we carried over from the conceptual phase? Do we have primary keys?	Make sure that every relationship has a primary key on one side of the relationship, and another primary key or a foreign key on the other side.

Answers may vary, but here's one possible logical model solution.

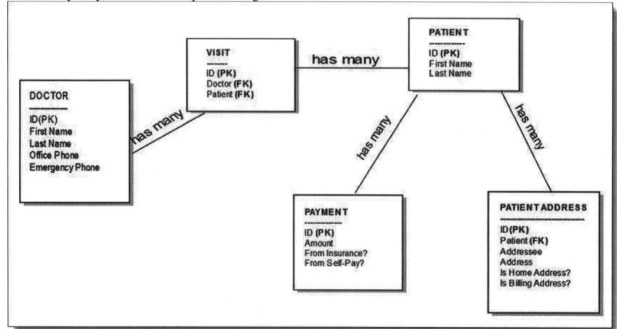

Note that we could expand on this by creating a separate entity for Addressee, the attribute in the Patient Address entity, to account for the fact that some patients may be receiving mail at an address with someone else's name (for example, a care facility, or living with relatives, etc.).

The physical model

You won't be creating objects in Access just yet. The physical model is still a *model*, although the model we end up with in this phase should look pretty close to what the tables will be eventually. This step is going to make our table design process pretty easy. We're going to:

- Use logical entities to create tables and fields.
    - Field placement in certain tables is still tentative until after we normalize.
- Decide on data types for each field based on what's available in the specific database we're using.

The physical model is probably what you're most familiar with if you haven't gotten involved in the database design process much. (When you look at Design View of a table in Access, you're seeing the realization of a physical model).

Keep in mind this can be an iterative process, in that we might need to loop through the modeling more than once (Either as a whole, or more frequently, just to re-do part of it). We might discover that some business requirements from our User Stories aren't covered in the logical model, so we the right pieces to that model and re-do the physical model based on the changes. Or there might be new requirements that show up when we present this model to our stakeholders—you know, the non-technical people. This is one of the benefits of modeling, actually: We have documents we can show to other people involved in the project, that they can understand and sign off on. This can save us from wasting a lot of time on creating an elegant solution that doesn't solve the problem!

Let's continue with our Customers database example. For each entity, ask yourself if each attribute might actually be multiple attributes. If so, this is the time to split it out into its individual fields. Consider the Customer entity from the logical model:

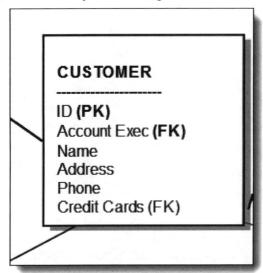

Let's go through each attribute and decide if it's a single value. If it is, we'll assign it a field name and a data type. If not, we'll split it out to individual fields and data types.

- **ID:** A single unique value. AutoNumber field if generating in database, Number or Text field is ID has been generated elsewhere and must be entered.
- **Account Exec**: Refers to an account executive, so this would be a single field of the same data type as the ID field in the Account Exec entity so that Access could create the relationship for us.
- **Address**: Multi-valued, so we should create multiple fields.
    - Street Address of data type Short Text

- City as data type Short Text
- State as data type Short Text (Limited to 2 characters if we're using standard US State abbreviations)
- Zip Code as data type Short Text (Limited to 10 characters for US Zip+4 format, as in "12345-6789"

- **Phone**: Possible multiple values, so we should consider a separate entity called Customer Phone here, with fields for a primary key, customer id, phone number and (optionally) what type of phone number is represented, like Office Phone, Home Phone, Mobile Phone, etc.
- **Credit Cards**: It's clear from this diagram that a customer could have multiple credit cards, so we should not represent this field in the physical design, and instead just have a foreign key in the Credit Cards entity that refers back to a Customer.

Our model evolves from the logical to the physical like this, then:

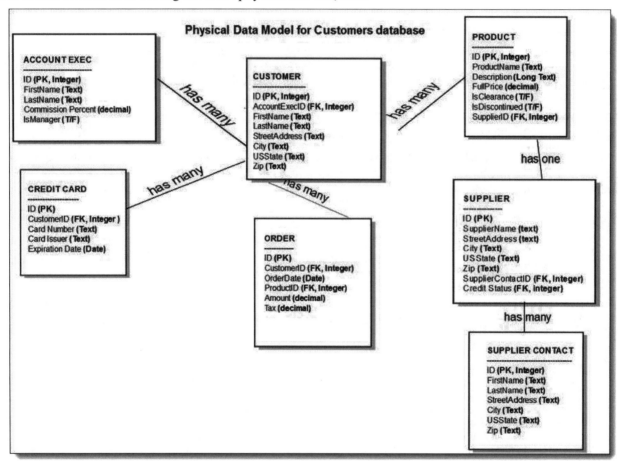

Notice that we have a new entity called Supplier Contact. Our logical model had a Supplier Contact attribute, and we've created an entity that recognizes the fact that there could be multiple supplier contacts, and created the new entity, with a foreign key left behind in the Supplier entity.

Exercise: Creating a physical model

Continue using the medical database example from the previous exercise, and create the physical data model from the logical one we did earlier. Here's a logical model to work from:

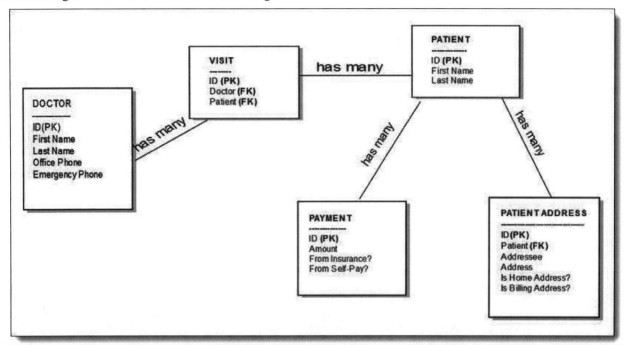

Do This	How & Why
1. For each entity, identify whether an attribute is a single value or multiple values.	Ask yourself: Does this attribute potentially contain multiple facts (That is to say, multiple pieces of information)? This could be either an attribute that naturally has multiple values like the first and last parts of someone's name, or an attribute that could contain multiple values of the same type like two phone numbers.
2. If an attribute is a single value, give it a field name and a data type.	Add the data type designation to the field.
3. If an attribute is multi-valued, decide what to do with it.	If it's a single fact but has multiple parts like an address, split the attribute into multiple fields in the same table. If it's a multi-valued attribute like a phone number, eliminate it from the entity. Create a new entity with a primary key, a foreign key to refer back to the original entity, and any other specific fields you need.
4. Look at your finished physical model. Check the keys to make sure all relationships are properly modeled, and that there's data types for each field.	

While answers may vary, here's one interpretation of the model so far:

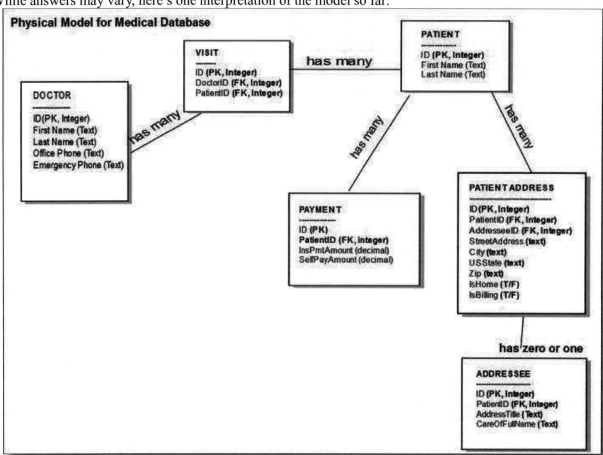

Notice that we chose to add a separate entity called Addressee to store the specific information about the details of a patient's address, given that they might be receiving mail at a care facility or a relative's or friend's residence. We don't care so much about the details of this other than making sure the mail gets to the right place, but you could add a more refined field set to the Addressee entity if you needed to. The important thing there is that some patient's addresses might have an addressee and some not, so we store the information separately to avoid a lot of null fields in our Patient Address entity.

Assessment: Fundamentals of good design

1. What two things does an ERD identify?

    - Relationships
    - Keys
    - Tables
    - Reports
    - Entities

2. The logical model adds what two things to the ERD?

    - Keys
    - Queries
    - Reports
    - Attributes
    - SQL

3. Which Model is closest to the finished database?

    - Conceptual
    - Physical
    - Representational
    - Logical

Module B: The normal forms

Technology changes quickly, no news there. In the world of relational databases though, our foundation for normalizing comes from Edgar Codd and his work for IBM in the 1970s in defining what's called *normal forms*. This is still the gold standard for how to define highly functioning non-redundant relational databases. Each normal form is a particular rule that applies to table design, and a modern database is considered to be fully normalized if it conforms to *third normal form* (3NF for short). A form is just another word for *rule* in this case. There are more normal forms, but it gets pretty theoretical after the third one, and most every business solution out there today only goes to 3NF.

You will learn:

- The goals of normalizing
- The first, second, and third normal forms

The goals of normalizing

We are designing here for relational databases that are considered transactional, in that we are optimizing for transactions (inserts, updates, deletes). By contrast, data warehousing databases are intentionally denormalized since they're used for reporting, not transactions. So, the rules we're discussing here wouldn't apply. We mention this just so that you know the rules only need to apply in so far as they serve you. Based on the way you use your data, it might be perfectly acceptable to denormalize your transactional database in some cases.

Let's take a look at the rule book here, and then explain what it means and how we can get our database to 3NF. Academic definitions of these forms tend to be a little too lofty. We'll do this in plain language.

First normal form

First Normal Form means that our table...

- Has a primary key, either one field, or a combination of multiple fields that when taken together constitute a unique value
- Has unique rows: No two rows contain exactly the same values
- Has unique columns, that is to say no columns that contain the same data
- Has records that do not contain more than one entry

Let's look at an example of an un-normalized table and see why we need to fix it and how we'd do that.

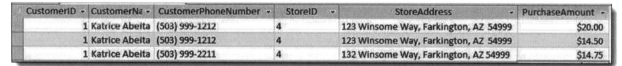

There are several problems: We don't have a primary key, so we're running into the possibility that we have exactly duplicated records. We're storing the customer's name and phone number in every record, leading to redundant data, and the possibility of data entry errors. Notice the phone number is different in the third record. Additionally, we have the Store ID and address in each record, so the store's address is repeated through each sale record, and again there are data entry errors.

To fix this to 1NF, we need to...

- Designate a primary key
- Put the customer data in its own table

- Put the store information in its own table
- Split the store address information into separate fields

So our new table designs might look like this instead:

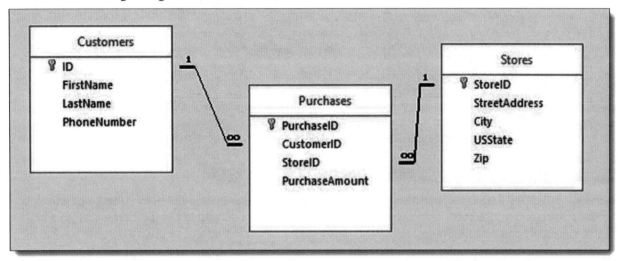

Since we have separate tables for Customers and Stores, the Purchases table now contains only the primary key, the foreign keys to refer back to Customers and Stores, and the specific details of the purchase. Now each Customer will be represented exactly one time in the Customers table, and each store will be represented exactly one time in the Stores table, with no redundancy and a more minimal chance of data entry errors.

Second normal form

Second Normal Form means that our table is normalized to 1NF, and additionally...

- In any table with a composite primary key, any non-key fields depend on the entire key.

A composite primary key means we've designated two or more fields that, when taken together, constitute a unique value. For example: Microsoft's Northwind sample database has an Order Details table, in which each record is a line item in a customer's order. The primary key is a composite, the combination of the OrderID and ProductID fields. Each product can only be ordered once per order though, so the combination of OrderID and ProductID is always unique.

When we say a field depends on the entire primary key, it only matters when there's a composite primary key. If we're using a single field primary key like Customer ID in a Customers table, then all the fields are by definition fully dependent on the primary key, and we don't have to worry, this part of 2NF is done!

Let's take an example of a table that isn't in 2NF yet:

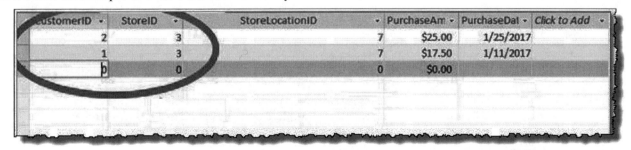

If we created the table above with a primary key of the first two fields, with the idea that together they would be unique, that's good so far. But the problem here is with the StoreLocationID field. It only depends on the StoreID field, not the CustomerID field. One way to check dependence it to just ask yourself: "If StoreLocationID changes, does it change the value of all the fields in the primary key?" In this case, it doesn't, because CustomerID is unaffected. So, this table does not make it to 2NF just yet.

One way to avoid this problem is to simply just not use composite primary keys, which is often easy to do since we have an AutoNumber field that will generate key values for us automatically. In some cases, this isn't practical, so let's keep our composite key from the example above and get this table to 2NF, like this:

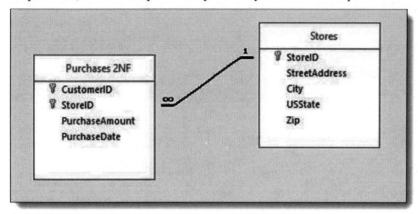

Even though we've retained the composite key in the Purchases table, notice that both remaining fields (Purchase Amount and Purchase Date) are completely dependent on both fields of the primary key, as each purchase is specific to a certain customer and a certain date.

Third normal form

Third Normal Form (3NF) means that the database is in 2NF, and additionally:

- Any non-key field provides a fact about the key.

Database guru Bill Kent provides this definition of third normal form in his essay "A Simple Guide to Five Normal Forms in Relational Database Theory" (Available at http://www.bkent.net/Doc/simple5.htm): "a non-key field must provide a fact about the key, the whole key, and nothing but the key."

3NF is violated when a non-key field is dependent on another non-key field. For example, take a look at this table:

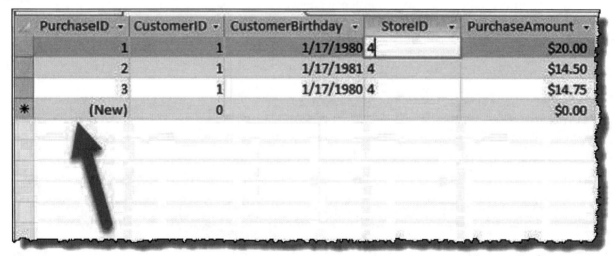

The CustomerBirthday field is dependent on the CustomerID field which is notably in this case not the primary key. CustomerBirthday is not a fact about the purchase, it's a fact about the customer. We've also get redundant data for the CustomerBirthday field and the possibility of data entry errors. The solution here is to put CustomerBirthday into the Customers table and not here.

Discussion: Normal forms

Answer the following questions about database designs with the sample tables shown here:

Field Name	Data Type
DoctorID	Number
DoctorName	Short Text
PatientID	Number
PatientName	Short Text
PatientBirthday	Date/Time
PatientPhoneNumbers	Short Text
LastVisitDate	Date/Time

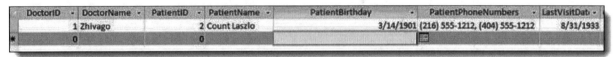

1. Does the table meet the requirements of First Normal Form? If not, what needs to be changed?

2. Assuming the table is already in 1NF, either because it naturally was or because you made changes, does the table meet the requirements of Second Normal Form? If not, what needs to be changed?

3. Now that we've gotten to 2NF, does the table meet the requirements of Third Normal Form? If not, what should we fix?

Assessment: Normal forms

1. No two rows having exactly the same data is part of which normal form?

   - 1st
   - 2nd
   - 3rd

2. Which normal form requires that Any non-key field provides a fact about the key?

   - 1st
   - 2nd
   - 3rd

Module C: Creating and modifying databases

After our database is planned out and your model is normalized, we could begin the process of creating tables, which leaves us with one more major task: deciding on the data type for each field.

You will learn about:

- Choosing field data types
- Constraints
- Changing table structure

Choosing data types

We may have done this at a high level in the physical modeling process. Obviously, all databases support the same basic data types, like numbers, strings of letters, dates and times, etc. But every database has a slightly different set of subtypes, so that's why we might wait until this point to decide on something more specific. Let's take a look at the common field data types in Access 2016 tables.

Numeric data types

For fields set to use the Number data type, Access 2016 provides subtypes that restrict the range and precision of the number. This is set using the Field Size property.

- *Byte*: Whole numbers from 0 to 255.
- *Integer*: Whole numbers from -32,768 to 32,767
- *Long integer*: Whole numbers from -2,147,483,648 to 2,147,483,647.
- *Single*: Floating point decimal numbers with up to 7 significant digits.
- *Double*: Floating point decimal numbers with up to 15 significant digits (Calculations use rounding in both Single and Double if there's too many digits for it to handle).
- *Decimal*: Numbers with up to 28 significant digits. Even though they're named Decimals, you can put integers in here to get around the upper limit of the Long Integer data type.
- *Currency*: A decimal with 4 digits to the right of decimal point and up to 15 on the left that's not rounded off during calculations.

Note: The *AutoNumber* data type is actually saved as a Long Integer, so when you're creating foreign keys to reference these fields, make sure you use the Long Integer data type.

String data types

Any time you want to store character data, which includes anything that has alphabetical characters, use one these two.

- *Short Text*: Any string up to 255 characters for Access desktop databases, with an upper limit below the 255-character max that you can set using the Field Size property. For Access web apps, you can adjust this up to 4000 characters. This field was called the *Text* data type before Access 2013.
- *Long Text*: Any string of 256 characters or more for desktop databases, and virtually unlimited for Access web apps (Unless you need more than 230 characters anyway!) This field was called the *Memo* data type before Access 2013)

Other data types

- *Date/Time*: Always saved in Access as a particular point in time, such as "January 20, 1941 5:00:00 AM". You can choose which part of this is displayed though, using the Format property of the field.

- *Yes/No*: Useful for any True/False data. Can be displayed as **Yes/No**, **True/False** or **On/Off** using the *Format* property of the field.

- *Calculated*: While it's not truly a data type on its own, setting the Data Type of an Access table field to Calculated will produce a handy dialog box that allows you to build an expression. The expression will dynamically produce a value using field from this table, other tables, and Access' own math, comparison, logical and/or string functions. You could even create your own function and use it here, too.

Constraints

Choosing a data type is a good first step for a table field. We don't want the word "tomorrow" showing up in a Date/Time field, do we? So, setting the data type takes care of that part. It's possible though, that not all the values allowed by a data type are valid for our particular type of data. If we're tracking student test scores on a 0 to 100 scale, for example, but the system allows negative values or values over 100 to be entered, eventually bad data will come up. Constraints help keep data entry people (or applications) from making the mistake.

Constraints come in many flavors, but you can consider anything that restricts the allowable values in a field to be a constraint. Technically, the Field Size properties we talked about setting for Data Types constitutes a constraint all on its own, Access just doesn't display that particular terminology.

Common constraints

The Field Properties list includes some common constraint settings:

- *Required*: A non-null value must be entered, so you can't leave the field blank in Datasheets or Forms when adding or updating a record.

- *Default Value*: Assigns a value to the field even if you don't. Setting a default value is a good way to make sure that there's something there for Required fields.

- *Validation Rule*: A property that allows you to build a custom expression limiting the value of a field. If you had a table tracking ATM withdrawals where only $20 bills were in the machine, you might limit the ATMWithdrawalAmount field to numbers divisible evenly by 20 with an expression like

```
ATMWithdrawalAmount Mod 20 = 0
```

and then set the companion *Validation Text* property to display an explanatory message if there was an attempt to store anything but an amount that was $20, $40, $60, etc.

Exercise: Creating a database

In this exercise, we're going to take a physical model and use it to create actual tables in an Access database with data types and validation rules. Use the physical model below as a guide for creating tables. Don't worry about the relationships yet, we'll take care of those in the next exercise.

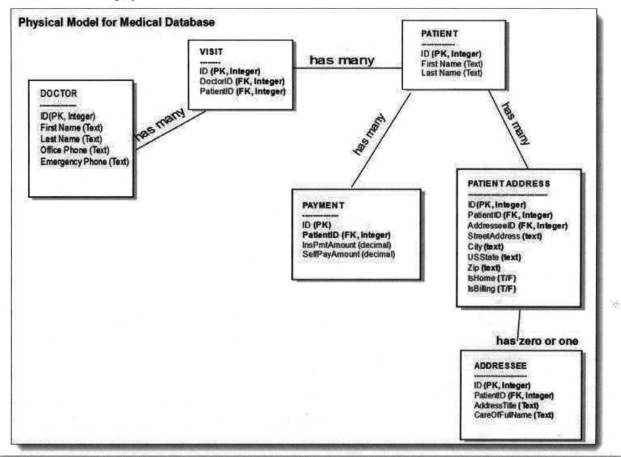

Do This	How & Why
1. Create a new Access database and name it `MedicalOffice`.	Save it in the current data folder.
2. On the Create tab, click **Table Design**.	
3. Add the fields from the Doctor table in the diagram. a) In the first Field Name, enter `ID`. b) From the first Data Type drop-down list, select **AutoNumber**. c) In the second Field Name, enter `FirstName` and make it **Short Text**.	 This will be the unique ID number for each record. Eliminate spaces in the name will make it easier to write queries.

Access 2016 Relational Database Design

Do This	How & Why
d) Enter the rest of the fields and data types for the Doctor table.	Use short text for text types. **Table1** | Field Name	Data Type
ID	AutoNumber
FirstName	Short Text
LastName	Short Text
OfficePhone	Short Text
EmergencyPhone	Short Text	
4. Right-click the ID field name and click **Primary Key**.	To make this the primary key field. A key will appear in the left column.
5. Click the save button, name the table `Doctor`, and click **OK**.	The table appears in the navigation pane.
6. Create the Visit table.	
a) Make the first field named `ID` as an **AutoNumber** data type.	
b) Make the second field DoctorID as a **Number** data type.	By default, it will be a long integer, which is necessary to match the AutoNumber type when you later add relationships.
c) Create the PatientID field, also as an integer number data type.	
d) Make ID the primary key.	
e) Save the table as Visit.	

7. Create the remaining tables in the diagram.
   • In each table, make `ID` and **AutoNumber** field and set it as the primary key.
   • Use **Short Text** as the data type for all text fields.
   • Use **Currency** as the data type for payment amount fields.
   • Use **Yes/No** as the field type for the fields listed as T/F.	

Do This	How & Why
8. Set the Required property for the required fields.	Select the field in table design view, and then in the general field properties, set Required to **Yes**. Set the following fields as required: • Doctor: FirstName, LastName, EmergencyPhone • Patient: FirstName, LastName • Visit: DoctorID, PatientID • Payment: PatientID • PatientAddress: Patient, and all Address-related fields • Addressee: All fields
9. Save and close all tables.	To close a table, click the X at the right end of the open objects tabs.

Changing table structure

Of course, you will probably need to make changes to the database structure after you've created it. The earlier you make changes, the better. Changing a field data type, for instance, after there are records in the table could result in lost data. Removing fields or changing field names after there are forms and queries will result in program errors.

Changing data types

You might find you need to change the data type of a field after there are records in the table. Even with the best modeling, requirements change. Probably the most common types of changes are of the Field Size variety. Maybe you've found that the Short Text field size is too restrictive, and you want to change to Long Text. In that case, no problem. Programmers would call this widening because we're converting to a less restrictive field size. Anything that already fit into a Short Text field would, by definition, convert to a Long Text.

Unfortunately, going back the other way with the conversion isn't so easy. If you try to convert back from Long Text to Short Text for example, Access will check your data and display a warning message if there are any field values that would be concatenated. You can choose at that point to continue with the operation or abort it.

The same idea applies to numeric fields. If you're converting from Integer to Long Integer, no problem in any case. But shortening from Long Integer to Integer will cause Access to check your data again and warn you if there's problems. In certain cases, the conversion might not be allowed, such as trying to convert a Text field to a numeric type if there's non-numeric characters in the Text.

Note that once a field is part of a relationship, as either a primary or foreign key, you cannot change its data type (or in the case of Number fields, its Field Size property).

Adding or deleting fields

You can add a field to a table at any time, and it's almost too easy. In Design View, just give it a name and a Data Type. In Datasheet view, click the Add New link that shows above the right-most existing field. Deleting a field could be more problematic, because you'd be deleting all the data in all the records of that table.

Access will always show a warning asking if you really want to do this, and this is your last chance to back off—Once you click Yes, the data is gone and the Undo button will not save you! Note that Access will not permit you to delete a field that's part of a relationship.

Exercise: Changing a database

In this exercise, we will add new fields to a table and change the data type of an existing field. The database MedicalOffice should be open.

Do This	How & Why
1. Open the Visit table in design view and add the following fields: • VisitDate (Date/Time) • VisitCharge (Currency) • DoctorNotes (Long Text)	
2. In the field properties for VisitDate, in Validation Rule, enter [VisitDate] <= Date()	To ensure a visit can't be made in the future.
3. Save and close the Visit table.	
4. Add at least one record to the Doctor table and one to the Patient table.	The ID will be an AutoNumber. Make up that names and numbers.
5. Add a record to the Visit table.	
a) The ID will AutoNumber. Use 1 for the Doctor and Patient numbers.	
b) Add a VisitDate in the future and try to tab to the next field.	You get a warning the value is prohibited. Change it to a valid value.
c) In the DoctorNotes field, enter enough text to exceeded 256 characters.	
6. Switch to the Design view for the Visit table.	
7. Change DoctorNotes to **Short Text** and click the Save button.	You get a warning that some data might be lost. That's because Short text is only 256 characters, and you have notes exceeding that.
8. Click **No**.	To avoid saving the table structure and return to Design view.
9. Close the Visit table without saving changes.	
10. Save and close the database.	

Assessment: Creating and modifying databases

1. What is the maximum size for a short text data type?
   - 16 characters
   - 255 characters
   - 1024 characters
   - 128 characters

2. What data type is an AutoNumber stored as?
   - Integer
   - Long integer
   - Single
   - Double

3. What constraint fills out a field with a given value even if you don't?
   - Base value
   - Required value
   - Default value
   - Valid value

4. True or false? You can't change a field from long text to short text if there is already text in a record.
   - True
   - False

Module D: Relationships and keys

It takes a while make sure your data is normalized. This results in a table structure that seems unnecessarily confusing to people who are new to relational databases, or who have used Microsoft Excel as a way to store data. The data is all scattered in multiple places. It can be a bit daunting, but it makes the database run as efficiently as possible. You bring all the data back together by leveraging the relationships we create between tables.

You will learn about:

- Keys
- Relationships
- Referential integrity

Parts of a relationship

Every relationship in every database exists between exactly two tables. Each table is potentially participating in many different relationships, but each individual relationship exists between a primary or unique key in one table, and a primary key, unique key or foreign key in another table.

Types of keys

A *primary key* is the field or fields that uniquely identifies a record. There is only one primary key per table in Access, and values cannot be null. An index is created on the primary key automatically. A unique key is a field or combination of fields that are unique. There can be as many unique keys as you want, and Access implements this as a unique index, meaning that the field values are copied and stored in a separate area to allow Access to return query results more quickly when the key fields are involved.

A *foreign key* is a field or combination of fields that link back to a primary or unique key in another table. If we had a Customers table with the primary key being the customer's unique ID, we'd see a foreign key column in the Orders table that had the customer's unique ID value in it. We use this primary key / foreign key relationship to bring back data from both tables in a query.

Types of relationships

There are 3 types of relationships in databases, and what type it is depends on the uniqueness of the data.

- A *one-to-one relationship* is when a primary or unique key in one table is joined in a relationship to a primary or unique key in another table. By definition here, there will be exactly one record on each side of the relationship. For example, if each of our customers is allowed to have one credit card on file, we could create a relationship between Customer ID in the Customers table and Customer ID in the CreditCards table.

- A *one-to-many relationship* is created when a primary or unique key is related to a foreign key that's not unique or primary. Even if you only end up with one record on the "many" side of the one-to-many relationship for some records, you're still allowed to add more records on the many side.

- A *many-to-many relationship* is unique here in that it actually involves creating a third table and relating it to the two existing tables. Remember our example about Doctors and Patients from the conceptual design phase? Let's say we've create tables for both of them. To create the many-to-many relationship, let's create another table we'll call *junction table* or a *bridge table*. This table "bridges the gap" between the two related tables. In the case of the example, we would probably create a table called Cases that would have foreign keys for both a Doctor and a Patient, along with the other fields related to that record of course.

Note: If you're looking at the relationship diagram in an Access 2016 database, look for a table that's the "many" side of 2 one-to-many relationships. There's your bridge table!

Referential integrity

Referential Integrity is making sure the information that links the smaller units of our data storage together are entered consistently, so that we can query our information reliably.

In Access, you create a relationship from the Relationships window. The requirement from Access is that the data types of the fields match. Unless you check the Enforce Referential Integrity box, you've created a relationship but not constrained the data in any way. There are some cases where you might want a relationship without referential integrity, but most often you want to check that box. Referential integrity guarantees that a value can't exist on the foreign key side that doesn't already exist on the primary/unique key side. For instance, it would prevent you from entering a Customer ID for a customer who doesn't exist.

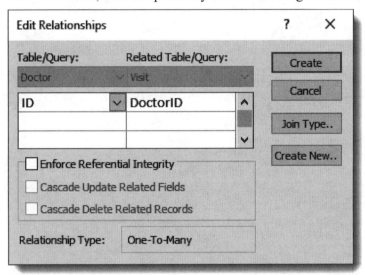

You're also deciding here what happens when the primary key field is updated, or the record is deleted. If you only check the **Enforce Referential Integrity** box and leave the other two unchecked, Access will maintain referential integrity for you in two ways: Once there are related records on the foreign key side, you won't be able to make changes to the primary/unique key value and you won't be able to delete the record. Referential integrity is maintained because there's always a matching value in the primary/unique field for any foreign key records.

If you check the **Cascade Update Related Fields** box, Access will still maintain referential integrity, but this time it will propagate the changed value on the primary/unique key side to all the records on the foreign key side.

If you check the **Cascade Delete Related Fields** box, you can see what's coming here, right? Access will once again maintain referential integrity, by deleting all the records with the same key value on the foreign key side when you delete the record containing the primary/unique key value. Caution is your friend here, as this can get rather messy. Consider that even though every relationship is between exactly two tables, the "many" side of our one-to-many relationship could be involved in relationships with other tables, where the Cascade Delete would cause problems. If that's the case, Access disallows the deletion.

Exercise: Creating table relationships

You'll create relationship between tables.

Do This	How & Why
1. Open the Medical Office database.	From the current data folder.
2. On the Database Tools tab, click **Relationships**.	To open the Relationships tab and the Show Table window. If the Show Table window isn't open, right-click a blank area of the Relationships area and click **Show Table**.
3. Add all tables to the Relationships area. a) Double-click each table, or select and click **Add**. b) When you have added all five tables, click **Close**.	

4. Drag the tables so that it will be easier to create and understand the relationships.

You can move them at any time for clarity.

Doctor
- ID
- FirstName
- LastName
- OfficePhone
- EmergencyPhone

Visit
- ID
- DoctorID
- PatientID
- VisitDate
- VisitCharge
- DoctorNotes

Patient
- ID
- FirstName
- LastName

Payment
- ID
- PatientID
- InsPmtAmount
- SelfPayAmount

Patient Address
- ID
- PatientID
- AddressID
- StreetAddress
- City
- USState

Addressee
- ID
- PatientID
- AddressTitle
- CareOfFullName

5. Create the first relationship. a) Drag the **ID** field in Doctor to the **DoctorID** field in Visit. b) Check **Enforce Referential Integrity**.	The Edit Relationships window opens.

Do This	How & Why
c) Click **Create**.	A relationship line appears with a 1 and an infinity sign.
d) Right-click the relationship line and click **Edit Relationship**.	You can edit or delete relationships after you create them.
e) Click **Cancel** to close the relationship window.	
6. Create the remaining relationships.	Drag the ID field from Patient to the PatientID fields in the other tables. Check **Enforce Referential Integrity** each time.
7. Open the Patient and Doctor tables in datasheet view.	Observe the ID numbers.
8. Open the Visit table and try to add a record using a doctor or patient ID that doesn't exist.	When you try to move to the next record, you get an error message.
9. Enter valid ID numbers.	
10. Save and close the database.	

Assessment: Relationships and keys

1. What uniquely identifies each record in a table?
   - Foreign key
   - Primary key
   - Referential integrity
   - One-to-many relationship

2. What prevents you from entering a foreign key value that doesn't refer to an existing record?
   - Primary key
   - Referential integrity
   - One-to-many relationship
   - Cascading updates

Summary: Database design

In this chapter, you learned about:

- The goals of good design and modeling, including conceptual, logical, and physical models.
- The goals of normalizing and about the 1st, 2nd, and 3rd normal forms.
- Choosing data types and constraints for fields and changing table structure.
- Relationships, keys, and referential integrity.
- Understand the basics of keys and indexes, and create and test basic table relationships.

Synthesis: Database design

If possible, split into groups of 2 to 4 people. You'll design and create a simple relational database.

1. Pick a project. It needs to be complex enough to require related tables but not so complex as to take too much time. For instance, a realistic database for a large retail store would require dozens of tables. Creating an inventory database for a small bookstore, though, might be feasible. Here are a few ideas:
   - Student records - classes, grades, schedule
   - Tutor database - students, tutors, session schedule, notes
   - Book store or music store inventory
   - Trucking/shipping - trucks, destinations, schedules
   - Tracking for any personal collection
2. Design a simple relational database.
   a) Write a use case and sketch out an ERD.
   b) Bring the design through conceptual, logical, and physical models.
      You'll have to make decisions on how to break down data so that it is normalized.
3. Create the database in Access.
   a) Create tables and decide on final data types and constraints.
   b) Create keys and relationships.
   c) Add some data to your tables.
4. Share and discuss your project with classmates.
   Discuss design choices, especially regarding normalization and relationships.

Chapter 3: Tables

You will learn how to:

- Create tables in Design view.
- Add fields in Datasheet and Table Design views.
- Add validation rules for fields and tables.
- Understand the basics of keys, indexes, and relationships.

Module A: Creating tables

Tables are where the data in your Access databases will live. Tables are just what they sound like: columns of types of data, called *fields*, and rows of related data, called *records*. There are various ways to create tables in Access, including using the Create Table button and using Table Design view.

You will learn how to:

- Create a basic table using the Table button on the Create tab.
- Create a table in Table Design view.

Creating a simple table

After you create a new, blank database, you will need to add tables to it in order to save data. Here is the simplest way to create a blank table:

1. Open a database or create a new one.
2. On the Create tab, click **Table**.

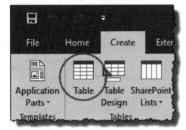

Access displays a datasheet view for your new table with an ID field. This is set by default to be an AutoNumber field, and it's also set as the *primary key* field. Change it if you want, but the AutoNumber is a usually a good choice for primary key, so some of your work is done.

Saving tables

After you create a new table, you should save it with a descriptive name.

1. With the Table open, click the Save button on the Quick Access toolbar.
   You can also press **Ctrl +S**.

2. Type a name for the table and click **OK**.
   Some database designers like to use a convention of having all objects of a certain type have the same prefix. So, you might call a table listing sales representatives, "tbl_reps".

Exercise: Creating a blank table

Do This	How & Why
1. Create a new Access 2016 database.	Open Access, click the Blank database tile, then click **Create**. This creates a new, blank database.
2. Save the database as `SalesDB`.	Click **File > Save As**, click **Access Database**, then click **Save As**. Close all objects if prompted, then save the database as "SalesDB" in the Tables folder.
3. Observe the list of objects.	There are currently no objects in this database. You'll create a table object.
4. On the Create tab, click **Table**.	The Table button is in the Tables group. Access opens a new table (Table1) in Datasheet view.
5. Observe the ID field	This is an AutoNumber field, meaning it will assign sequential number to each row, or record, that is added to the table.
6. Save the table as `Companies`.	Click the Save button on the Quick Access toolbar, type "Companies," and click **OK**. The table is now named, "Companies."

Access 2016 Relational Database Design

Creating tables in Design view

By creating a table in Table Design View, you can start with the same AutoNumber type ID field, but you'll have many more options in the Field Properties window on the bottom of the screen.

Feel free to switch back and forth between Datasheet and Table Design view when working on the table. In either view, you will have access to the Table Tools group on the Table tab of the ribbon. You can set table properties here, including the default sort order, and filtering to display only certain rows. The Relationships button will also show you existing relationships in your database, and give you a chance to create a relationship for the table you're working on.

To create a table in Table Design view, click the **Table Design** button on the Create tab.

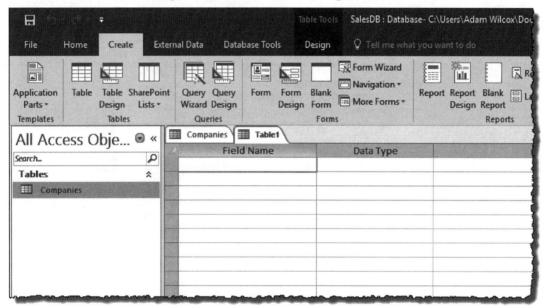

Exercise: Creating a table in Design view

Do This	How & Why
1. On the Create tab, click **Table Design**.	The SalesDB database should be open in Access.
2. Observe the new table in Table Design view.	Table Design view shows a grid you can use to create the fields in a table. The Table Tools Design ribbon tab is active.
3. Attempt to save the new table.	Click the Save button. You get an error because the table does not yet have any fields and cannot be saved.
4. Click **OK**.	You'll save the table later after creating a field in it.

Assessment: Creating tables

1. You can create tables only in Table Design view. True or false?

   - True
   - False

2. Which of the following are examples of table properties? Select all answers that apply.

   - Sort order
   - Primary key
   - Filtering
   - Relationships

Module B: Creating fields

Fields are the types of data that your tables contain. For example, a list of employees might have a text field called txt_firstname for the employees' first names, and a data field, dt_birthdate, for their birthdates. There are many ways to create fields in Access.

You will learn how to:

- Create fields in Datasheet view.
- Create fields in Table Design view.

Creating fields in Datasheet view

In Datasheet view, you can always use the Click to Add button, just to the right of the last field you created.

1. Click the **Click to Add** button.

    This is just to the right of the last field in the view.

    A drop-down prompting you to choose a Data Type for your field.

2. Select a data type for the field.
3. Rename the field by double-clicking its heading.
4. Configure other properties by using the Fields tab in the Table Tools section of the ribbon.

As you'd expect, anything you do in Datasheet view shows up in Table Design view and vice versa. You'll see many of the same options in Table Design View, but many users find this to be a more comfortable interface.

Exercise: Adding a field in Datasheet view

SalesDB is open.

Do This	How & Why
1. Open Companies in Datasheet view.	Double-click the Companies table in the Navigation pane.
2. Create a Short Text field called `CompanyName`.	
a) Click **Click to Add**.	It is to the right of the ID field heading. 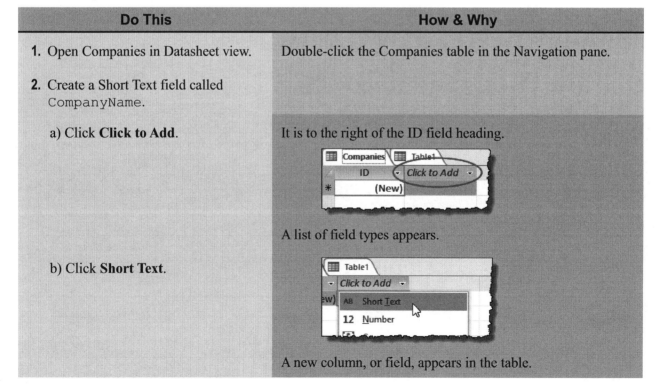 A list of field types appears.
b) Click **Short Text**.	A new column, or field, appears in the table.

Do This	How & Why
c) Name the new field `CompanyName`.	Double-click the heading, type `CompanyName`, then press **Enter**.
3. Create a Short Text field called `NYSESymbol`.	Click **Click to Add**, click **Short Text**, then rename the field by double-clicking its heading.
4. Add the following fields: • Data type: `Hyperlink`, Field name: `Website` • Data type: `Short Text`, Field name: `TwitterHandle` The table should look like this now. *[Screenshot of Companies table with columns: ID, CompanyNa, NYSESymbol, Website, TwitterHand]*	
5. Save the table.	Click the Save button.
6. Switch to Table Design view.	On the Home tab, click **View**, then click **Design View**. Notice that the ID field is already designated as a primary key, and that all your field data types have been carried over from Datasheet view.

Creating fields in Table Design view

In Design View, the process of adding fields is similar.

1. In a blank row, give the field a name.
2. Select a data type. (You can have up to 255 fields in any one table.)

Field properties in Design view

As you add fields, there will be a full set of options in the Field Properties. Some properties are common to all data types. Required, for example, ensures that users must enter a value. You can use Caption to set a friendly caption for the field that shows as a label in Datasheet view.

Some fields will give you different property choices. If you add a Number field, the Field Size property gives you a drop-down choice of different types of numbers, including whole numbers, fractions, or a range of allowable values. Integer and Long Integer support different maximum and minimum values. However, if you create a Short Text field, the Field Size property will show the value 255 by default. In this case, you're setting the maximum number of characters allowed in that field, up to 255 for desktop databases.

Setting a primary key field

Every table should have a primary key. When you create a table in Datasheet view, the ID field that is created automatically is set as a primary key. When you create a table in Design view, you have to designate a primary key field yourself.

1. Click in the field you want to designate a primary key.
2. On the Table Tools Design tab, click **Primary Key**.

Exercise: Adding fields in Table Design view

The SalesDB database is open.

Do This	How & Why
1. Open Table1 in Design view.	Click its tab. There aren't yet any fields in this table.
2. Add an AutoNumber field called `ID`.	
a) Under Field Name, type ID.	In the first row of the table. In Design view, each row represents a single field.
b) Under Data Type, select **AutoNumber**.	To create an AutoNumber field. Notice that the properties in the bottom pane change based on the selection of field type.
3. Set the ID field as the primary key.	
a) Click in the row for the ID field.	
b) On the Table Tools Design tab, click **Primary Key**.	A key icon appears on the row button for the field.
4. Enter the rest of the fields as shown.	(Field Name / Data Type: ID / AutoNumber; CompanyID / Number; StreetAddress / Short Text; City / Short Text; Region / Short Text; PostalCode / Short Text; Country / Short Text; IsHeadquarters / Yes/No; MainPhone / Short Text; DateOpened / Date/Time)
5. Save the Table as `Locations`.	Click the Save button and enter the name.

Do This	How & Why
6. View Locations in Datasheet view.	Click **Views** > **Datasheet View**. In Datasheet view, each field is represented by a column.

The Locations table in Datasheet view

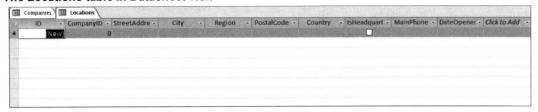

Assessment: Creating fields

1. In which view can you enter field data? Choose the one correct answer.

   - Datasheet view
   - Table Design view

2. How many fields can you have in a single table? Choose the one correct answer.

   - 10
   - 12
   - 144
   - 255

3. Which of the following are properties that are common to all field types? Select all correct answers.

   - Required
   - Decimal places
   - New values
   - Caption

4. When you create a new table, Access always assigns a default primary key. True or false?

   - True
   - False

Module C: Data Validation

Data validations ensures that your tables contain valid data. Valid data is data that your database can use to get the results you intend. There are many types of validation, both for fields and for tables.

You will learn how to:

- Identify the purpose of data validation.
- Control validation through the use of field properties.
- Test validations.
- Control table-level validation.

The purpose of validation

There's one reason to do data validation: To make sure we have valid data.

Seems obvious, right? It is. But you've probably seen applications where this has been ignored. If you've ever had to manually go through a spreadsheet to verify that everyone put the data in the way they were supposed to, you know why data validation is important. You will also understand why you should make it as automatic as possible. You don't want to depend on someone knowing what sort of data to put in; you want the database to enforce those rules and not allow bad data.

The best place to start with data validation is within tables. There are times when it's appropriate to do some validation in a form as well. But when you create rules for your table fields, it doesn't matter how or where your data is used, those rules are the "last line of defense," and will always be enforced. It doesn't matter whether someone is using a form, or trying to manipulate the data from a web app, your validation rules are there protecting your data.

Data validation using field properties

Many types of validation can be set by using field properties.

Required fields Setting Required to Yes forces a non-null value to be entered in a field. This property does not appear for the AutoNumber field, since the value is automatically entered when the record is created.

Default values Shows the value you enter in Datasheet view or in Forms when a new record is being created. While not technically a validation property, think of it as giving your users a clue to what format of data you're looking for. If you've set Required to Yes, then setting a Default Value ensures that there is at least this default value in the field. You can also be dynamic here, in that the Default Value can be the result of a function. Want Date/Time fields to default to today's date? This is where you can do it.

Format	
Input Mask	
Caption	
Default Value	Date()
Validation Rule	

Allow zero length Text-based fields like Short Text and Long Text include this property. Setting it to Yes allows empty strings to be stored for the field. If you set both Required and Allow Zero Length to Yes, Access will store a zero-length string for the field instead of a null value. This can be helpful as the display of a zero-length string can be changed using the Format property.

Validation rules A *Validation Rule* allows you to set a property using a custom expression that limits the value of a field. Validation text gives information about your rules to users.

Testing validation

You can test to make sure all data in a table conforms to the validation rules, as well as to Required and Allow Zero Length property settings. On the Table Tools Design tab, click **Test Validation Settings** to general a report. If there's lots of data in the table, this could take a while.

Exercise: Setting the Required and Default Value properties

In this exercise, you'll set fields as required, then create a default value for a field.

Do This	How & Why
1. Open the Companies table in Design view.	If necessary. You'll set two fields as required in this table.
2. Set CompanyName as a required field.	
a) Click within the row for the field.	
b) In the Properties list, set Required to **Yes**.	Click the drop-down arrow at the right of the property box, then click **Yes**.
3. Set the Website field as required.	A quick way to do this is to double-click Required on the left in the Properties pane. Double clicking the name of a field with a drop-down list will cause Access to cycle through its values. For example, double-clicking the Field Size property of a Number field will cycle through the available sub-types.
4. Save the table.	
5. Open the Locations table in Design view.	
6. Set the default value for the DateOpened field to today's date.	
a) Click within the DateOpened field row.	
b) Click in the Default Value property.	
c) Type `Date()`, then press **Enter**.	
7. Save the table.	

Setting validation rules

Setting a validation rule can seem complicated. You need to have an expression, plus text to communicate what the rule does and what to do if the rule is violated. But Access has a window that guides you through the process.

1. Select the field for which you want to create a validation rule.
2. Click the ellipsis button at the end of the field's Validation Rule property box.
    This will display the Expression Building window.
3. Use the Expression Builder to build a validation expression.
    - Expand the Functions list to choose a category and a function.
    - Expand the Constants list to select constants such as True, False, and Null.
    - Expand the Operators list to select arithmetic and logical operators.

A validation expression to test that the HireDate is before today's date

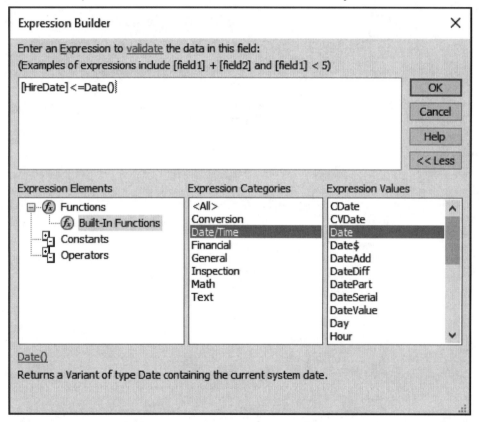

4. Use the Validation Text property to provide a message to users about what type of data your validation rule will enforce. Setting Validation Rule is technically all that's needed to make the rule be enforced. You should also set the Validation Text property, though. Since there could be many different validation errors, it's always helpful to include the Display name of the field in the Validation Text message to guide them to the right place to make the change.

Exercise: Setting validation rules

In this exercise, you'll set validation rules to restrict the country that is entered,

Do This	How & Why
1. Open the Locations table in Design view.	If necessary. Our fictional sales company has business permits only for the United States, Canada and Mexico. You'll create a validation rule that accepts only those values in the Country field of the Locations table.
2. Create a validation rule to restrict the Country field.	
a) Click in the row for the Country field.	
b) Click the ellipsis for the Validation Rule property.	On the right of the property box. This opens the Expression Builder window.
c) Enter the code shown.	`[Country]="USA" or [Country]="Canada" or [Country]="Mexico"`
d) Click **OK**.	
3. Enter validation text for the field.	
a) In the Validation Text field, enter, `The country must be USA, Canada, or Mexico.`	
4. Save the table.	
5. Test the validation rule.	
a) View the Locations table in Datasheet view.	

Do This	How & Why
b) In the first row, enter an invalid country.	Access displays a message with your validation text. 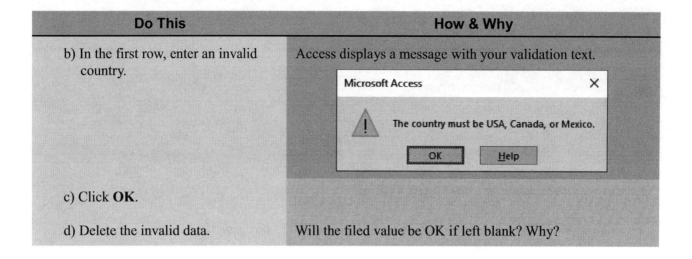
c) Click **OK**.	
d) Delete the invalid data.	Will the filed value be OK if left blank? Why?

Setting table-level validation

Field validation applies only to one field, and validation rules for fields can't refer to other fields. But what about the cases where one value in a record is dependent on another? That's when you will need to create table-level validation rules.

This validation rule can have multiple conditions, but there is only one rule per table allowed from here. Doing more than one rule at this level would require a code-based solution that's beyond the scope of this course. Keep in mind you're going to have a Validation Text message related to the error, so try to keep the Validation Rule to one specific condition.

There are a couple of ways to enter table-level validation rules.

1. Display the expression Builder for the table-level validation rule.
   - In Design view, display the Property Sheet for the table, and then click the ellipsis next to the table's Validation Rule property.
   - In Datasheet view, on the Table Tools Fields tab, click **Validation > Validation Rule**.
2. Use the Expression Builder to build a validation expression for the table. You can refer to multiple fields.
3. Enter Validation Text for the table.
   You can do this by accessing the property in either of the ways you accessed the table's Validation Rule property.

Exercise: Creating a table-level validation rule

Our fictional company did not receive a permit to do business with its Mexico location until 2010. You'll create a Validation Rule at the table level to enforce this rule, since the rule has to consider values from two different fields.

Do This	How & Why
1. Show the Properties sheet for the Locations table.	On the Table Tools Design tab, click **Property Sheet**.
2. Open the Expression Builder for the table's Validation Rule property.	Click in the validation rule box in the table's property sheet, then click the ellipsis button.
3. Enter the expression as shown.	This expression checks both the Country and DateOpened fields, which you can do only with table-level validation. ([Country]="Mexico" And [DateOpened]>=#1/1/2010#) or ([Country]="USA") or ([Country]="Canada")
4. Click **OK**.	To enter the validation rule.
5. Enter a validation text message for the rule.	Click in the Validation Rule box for the table's properties, and enter an appropriate message.
6. Delete the validation rule and message for the Country field.	In the field properties, not the table properties. You no longer need this rule.
7. Save the table.	When you do so, Access gives you a message about data integrity. Click **Yes**. Because you've entered some testing data, some of that data may violate the current rules. Click **Yes** to close these messages.
8. Test the new rule.	Go to Datasheet view, and then enter a record with a Country of Mexico, but an OpenedDate before January 1, 2010. Your validation text for the table-level rule appears.
9. Dismiss the message and fix the data.	You might need to try a couple of times.

Do This	How & Why
10. Verify that you can still enter USA or Canada regardless of the data.	Try a couple of dates, before and after January 1, 2010, for each country.
11. Delete any records you may have created in the Locations table.	
12. Save the table.	

A table-level validation text message

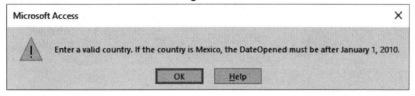

Assessment: Data validation

1. It is generally better to perform validation on tables rather than on forms. True or false?
   - True
   - False

2. You always use field properties to perform data validation in tables. True or false?
   - True
   - False

3. Default values for fields cannot be changed by the user when entering data. True or false?
   - True
   - False

4. Which of the following would you use to display a message to users while entering data? Select the one correct answer.
   - Validation text
   - Caption property of a field

Module D: Relationships and keys

Key fields allow for the uniqueness of records and for quick searching of your tables. They are also important to creating relationships between tables. And table relationships are the key to unlocking the power of a relational database such as those in Access.

You will learn how to:

- Describe the importance primary keys in indexing and relationships.
- Create unique indexes.

The importance of primary keys and indexes

Access uses *primary keys* for two major purposes: to guarantee the uniqueness of records, and to allow quick searching of the records in a table.

Access automatically creates an *index* on the primary key field. You can optionally create indexes that include other fields, and you'll frequently do this to satisfy the requirements of the queries you run most often. The more records a table contains, the more crucial an index is to quick retrieval of records. The index is a separate section of storage that Access creates. Think of it like a glossary in a book. If you want to find a particular word or subject in the book, you go to the Glossary, find the word or subject in alphabetical order, and the glossary refers you to a specific page number in the book.

Access uses indexes the same way. When you create an index on a field or combination of fields, Access maintains this separate storage through inserts, updates, and deletes. When you run a query that returns records, Access will automatically choose the best index to use. "Best," in this case, means the one that gets things done the fastest. The index contains pointers to where the record that satisfies the query is located in the database (The same way a Glossary in a book contains numbers that "point" you to pages in the book). This prevents Access from having to scan records that are out of the index's range.

Let's say you create a query that returns records between a certain range of dates. If you've indexed the date field of the table you're querying, Access can go find the earliest date you're looking for in its index, then go get the records the index points to until it hits the index value that has the latest date you're looking for. Since the index is automatically sorted, the query runs very efficiently because never has to look at a record in the table that doesn't match your requirements.

Why data type matters

Since the primary key field is automatically indexed, Access is essentially copying that field's value to the index it creates for the field. The smaller the size of the index field, the quicker Access can scan the index and find the records you want. To take an extreme example of what *not* to do, imagine that you created a primary key whose Data Type was Long Text (you should almost never use this data type, by the way). Access wouldn't find this very efficient as it would take more time to scan the index than it would just to find the actual records themselves.

This is why most often, primary keys are numeric fields and they rarely or never change. Their storage size is small and lets Access efficiently scan many index rows. More unique values in an index is best (using a Yes/No as an index isn't really going to help you much), but there's a reason Access suggests the AutoNumber field as the default primary key. It's a Long Integer data type, so it's easy to catalog into its internal indexes. This also means that when you create relationships, the foreign key values from other tables that refer back to the primary key will be similarly compact in storage size.

If a primary key value needs to change and is part of a relationship with another table, you'll need to enable the ability for the key value to change. In the Relationships window, you can click **Cascade Update Related Fields**, which will cause Access to change the values for the foreign key records table when the primary key changes. You can also click **Cascade Delete Related Records**, which will cause Access to attempt to delete the entire record on the foreign key table when that value is deleted from the primary key table, so be careful!

The default behavior of Access is to simply not allow a change to the primary key field value when there is an existing relationship using that key.

Creating primary keys

You can change the primary key from the default AutoNumber ID field Access provides.

To create a multi-column primary key, simply highlight all the fields you want to include and click the same button.

1. Remove the primary key designation from the ID field.
   In Table Design view, click within the ID field and then click **Primary Key** in the Tools section of the ribbon.
2. Highlight the field or fields you want to make into the new primary key or keys, then click **Primary Key**. Be aware that multi-column keys increase the complexity of your relationships, because you'll have to have matching multi-column foreign keys. In a majority of tables, it's usually easier and more efficient to stay with the AutoNumber ID field as the primary key.

Exercise: Discussing primary keys

Do This	How & Why

1. Your team is importing data from an Excel spreadsheet. The formulae used in the spreadsheet employed a combination of a customer's last name, city and state to guarantee the uniqueness of the record.
 	
   a) Why or why isn't this a good candidate for the primary key in the Access table you're importing the data to?
 	
   b) If it isn't, what should you do instead?	

2. An AutoNumber field assigns a consecutively incremented integer to new records. When might it be appropriate to use a numeric field for the primary key but not use the AutoNumber functionality?	

Do This	How & Why
3. Your Order Line Item table has a composite primary key consisting of the order id and product id. If you create a table that's related to Order Line Item, what fields or fields should the foreign key reference? • Order ID only • Product ID only • Both Order ID and Product ID if the related table has both order and product information • Both Order ID and Product ID because that's your only choice.	

Deciding whether you need unique indexes

Sometimes you have data that is or should be naturally unique, but for a variety of reasons you don't want to use it as a primary key. That's what a unique index is for. While you will almost always have a primary key for a table, unique indexes are optional. A table can have only one primary key, but you can create as many unique indexes as you need per table. Each index can include up to 10 fields.

Consider information that's naturally unique but sensitive; generally, you wouldn't use such data as a primary key field because you don't want that information spread around to other tables. You should limit such data to being in only one table and protect that table from users who shouldn't see it. But if the data is unique in the real world, you should have a rule that keeps it unique in the database. If there's a combination of fields that need to be unique when combined, you can also create a unique index.

Creating unique indexes

Here is how to create a unique index.

1. In Table Design view, click **Indexes** on the Table Tools Design tab.
2. Enter a name for the index in the next available row of the Index Name column.
3. Set Unique Values to **Yes**, then choose up to 10 fields in the Field Name column.
    You enter additional fields for a key in additional rows, but don't add a new Index Name in those rows.
4. Close the Indexes window.

The following Index table, for example, has 3 indexes: A default Primary Key index on the DoctorID field; a unique index for FirstName, LastName, and EmergencyPhone together (with the Unique property set to Yes); and another single field index for OfficePhone.

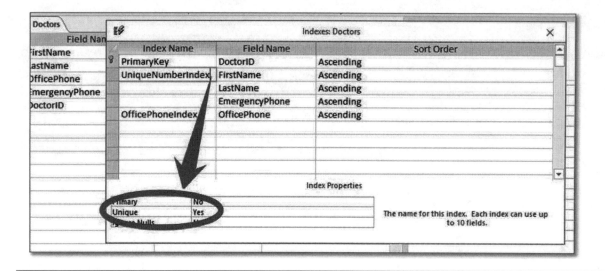

Exercise: Discussing unique indexes

Do This	How & Why
1. Considering the data you work with, identify fields on which it would be appropriate to create a Unique index when those fields aren't or shouldn't be primary keys.	Common answers might include: • Social Security number • Driver's License number • Multi-column indexes on any combination of columns that should be unique.

Creating relationships

You create relationships between tables by associating primary keys in one table to foreign keys in another. You do this in the Relationships window.

1. Open a table, then click the **Relationships** on the Database Tools tab.

    This will open the Relationships window in which you can see all the relationships in your database no matter which table you were just working on.

2. If the tables you want to be related aren't showing, right-click a blank part of the window and click **Show Table**.

    When you double-click a table, you'll see it appear in the window with the Show Table window staying open. Notice that you can also create relationships that incorporate queries, but this is rare.

3. To relate fields in two tables, drag a field or fields from one table and drop on the matching field or fields in the second table.

    Access will attempt to figure out the relationship type based on the data types of the fields and whether one or both is part of a primary or unique key. If that fails, you'll see the word "Indeterminate" under the Relationship Type section of the dialog box. Usually this means you're trying to relate fields in which neither side is part of a primary or unique key. Access won't end up allowing this to be a relationship, so check which fields you're including and try again.

4. Close the Relationships window when you're finished.

It's also a requirement to have the same number of fields with the same data types on both sides of the relationship.

If you want, you can choose to hide the display of a relationship by right-clicking on a table and clicking **Hide Table**. The relationship will continue to exist, though, and the referential integrity that goes with it will still be enforced.

Exercise: Creating table relationships

In this exercise, you'll create a new table in your database and then create relationships among the tables.

Do This	How & Why
1. Create a new table in Design view as shown.	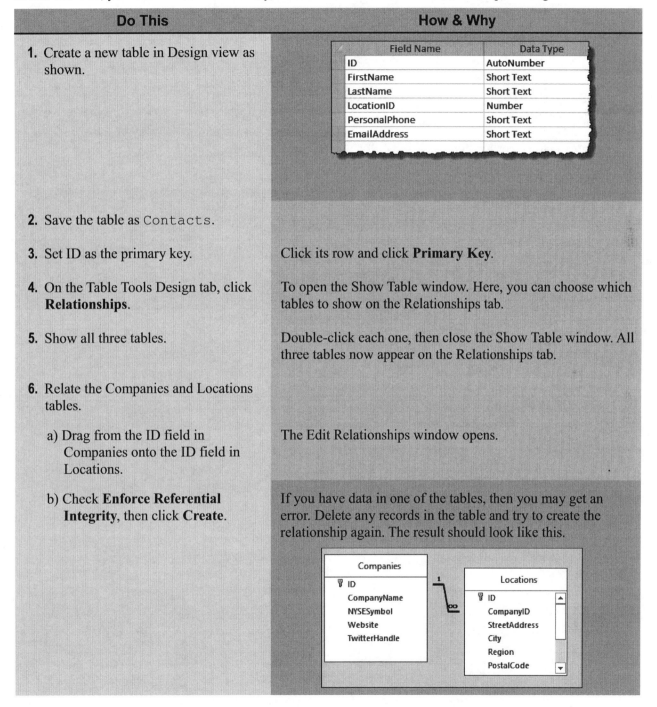
2. Save the table as `Contacts`.	
3. Set ID as the primary key.	Click its row and click **Primary Key**.
4. On the Table Tools Design tab, click **Relationships**.	To open the Show Table window. Here, you can choose which tables to show on the Relationships tab.
5. Show all three tables.	Double-click each one, then close the Show Table window. All three tables now appear on the Relationships tab.
6. Relate the Companies and Locations tables.	
a) Drag from the ID field in Companies onto the ID field in Locations.	The Edit Relationships window opens.
b) Check **Enforce Referential Integrity**, then click **Create**.	If you have data in one of the tables, then you may get an error. Delete any records in the table and try to create the relationship again. The result should look like this.

Do This	How & Why
7. Relate the Locations and Contacts tables as shown.	Drag from the ID field in Locations to the LocationID field in Contacts, check Enforce Referential Integrity, and click **Create**. 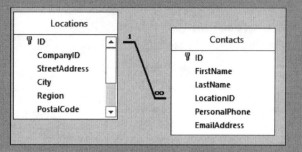
8. Test the relationships.	
a) Enter a new record in the Companies table.	Note the ID number Access generates.
b) Enter a new record in the Locations table.	Use the ID number you noted before as the CompanyID value. If you use a CompanyID that does not exist as an ID in the Companies table, you will not be able to save the record.
c) Enter a new record in the Contacts table.	This time, try using a LocationID value that does not exist in the Locations table's ID field. You get an error because the database is enforcing referential integrity. 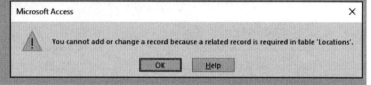
d) Click OK, then enter a valid LocationID.	As long as the value exists in the Locations table's ID field, you will be able to save the record.
9. Close the database, saving your changes to the relationships.	

Assessment: Relationships and keys

1. You can change the primary key in a table from the AutoNumber ID field to some other field. True or false?

    - True
    - False

2. A primary key can be based on which of the following? Select the single best answer.

    - Only on a single field.
    - On one or a combination of two fields.
    - On any number of fields in the table.

3. Is it appropriate to use social security numbers as a primary field?

    - Yes
    - No

Summary: Tables

In this chapter, you learned how to:

- Create and save simple tables in Datasheet and Design view.
- Add fields in Datasheet view; add fields and control their properties in Table Design view; and specify a primary key.
- Add and test validation rules for fields and create table-level validation rules that use combinations of fields.
- Understand the basics of keys and indexes, and create and test basic table relationships.

Synthesis: Tables

1. Create a new Database.
   Call it `TablesSynDB` and store it in the current chapter folder.
2. Create a new table called **Teachers** with the following fields:
   - ID: AutoNumber
   - FirstName: Short Text
   - LastName: Short Text
   - Specialty: Short Text
3. Make the FirstName and LastName fields Required.
4. Create a validation rule for the Specialty field that accepts only these entries:
   - Math
   - Science
   - Language Arts
   - History
   - Music
   - Dance
5. Create an appropriate validation text message for the rule.
6. Test the table, properties, and rule by entering a couple of sample records.
   Try both valid and invalid entries for the Specialty field.
7. OPTIONAL: Try making the Specialty field a list instead of Short Text with validation.
   From the Data Type list for the field, select Lookup Wizard and follow the steps. After using the wizard, use the Row Source property on the Lookup tab of the field's properties to enter the values. This is a better approach to this kind of thing in general, because it will restrict users to valid entries.
8. Create a second table called **Classes** with the following fields:
   - ID: AutoNumber
   - ClassTitle: Short Text
   - TeacherID: Number
9. Relate the ID field in the Teachers table to the TeacherID field in the Classes table, enforcing referential integrity.
   You'll need to close the tables before creating the relationships.

10. Text the referential integrity of the relationship.
    Try entering a record in the Classes table that does not have an associated TeacherID in the Teachers table.
11. Close all windows and the database.

The relationship created in the Synthesis exercise

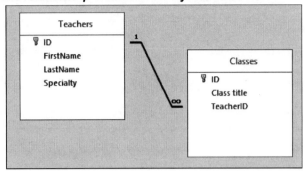

Chapter 4: Queries

You will learn:

- About basic queries
- How to modify queries
- How to use calculated fields in queries

Module A: Creating basic queries

Tables are the foundation of your database, where all the data is stored. Almost equally as important though, is your catalog of queries.

You will learn:

- About query types
- How to create Select queries
- How to create Action queries

What is a query?

It's a given that you will want to use your data in forms and reports, but often you only want to select certain fields or records instead of an entire table. Instead of creating these in an ad hoc manner, redefining the data source each time, you can create a *query* object which itself can serve as a data source. If you later want to change it, you can change the query once and have it be reflected in all the places it's being used as a data source. You can also create queries to automate common data tasks, like adding data to an existing table, creating a new table, or doing updates to existing data.

One of the great benefits of a query is that it's dynamic, in that every time you run it, you're getting exactly the set of records that's in the database at that time. In fact, the returned records from a query are often referred to as a recordset. When you define a query, you're creating the question (which is to say, a SQL statement) that is asked (executed) when you request it. This means the information is always as accurate as the query definition.

Access supports two main types of query:

- Select queries
- Action queries

Select queries

Far and away the most often used type of query is the select query. If your database is live, online and being actively used, you're probably adding new records as well as updating and deleting existing ones. If you were to track overall database activity, though, the vast majority of work done by the database engine is to return recordsets from queries. Access 2016 provides a wide variety of useful query types to return data, all of which you can create directly from a query design window. Technically, you're creating SQL statements that Access will execute, but you will probably be able to do most of your query design work without ever having to directly code up any SQL syntax.

For purposes of clarity, this course defines a Select Query as any query that should return a recordset. This could be as simple as getting some subset of the fields in a table, or adding some filtering so that we get only a certain set of records that match a condition. It could even be adding some formatting to fields so they display in a more user-friendly way to someone who's viewing the query results in a report. This way you have complete control over what data is returned and how that data looks. In Select queries, table data isn't changed: you're simply choosing some set of data from a table or tables and creating a dynamic recordset.

Action queries

Action queries are called that because they do something. Specifically, they do something that affects a table, either by altering existing ones or creating new ones. For example: Maybe you'd like someone to have a snapshot of some table's data, but without access to some fields (like sensitive personal information). You could create a table with a Make Table query that only contains a subset of fields. Maybe you're bringing data in from some external source like a SQL Server database, or an Excel spreadsheet, and you want to add it to an existing table. There's where an Append query does the job.

In fact, if you're thinking about the basic functions you can perform to manipulate data, there are Action queries for all 3 types. An Append query does inserts, an Update query does updates, and a Delete query does deletes. Again, you're working from a query design window here without having to get involved with the actual SQL syntax that the query executes, and in the same way as Select queries, Action queries are dynamic in that they are acting on the data where it is at the time the query executes. While Select queries are often the data source for forms and reports, this is not the case with Action queries; their mission is to perform their action rather than to provide a recordset.

Getting Started with basic Select queries

In this section, you will create queries that return records. You'll start by getting to know the query design window, then how to add tables to use in the query, then add fields to display results, and finally test your query design by executing the query and seeing the resulting datasheet. No matter what your intended eventual use for the query you're designing, you always start with the goal of seeing the recordset. This ensures that we have an accurate set of records when we want to use the query as the data source for a form or report.

The Query Design window

To create a new query, go to the Create tab on the ribbon. You can choose the **Query Wizard** button and have Access walk you through the query creation process, or pick the **Query Design** button to go directly to the query design window. Either way you choose, you'll eventually end up in the query design window. The Wizard is just an easy way to get started; after you go through the initial steps, you'll have the opportunity to manually edit anything about the query you want.

Tip: If you're a little unsure about how to get started, use the Query Wizard to design a query and note how your choices affect the results. After a while it'll be easier to see how to design a query on your own from scratch.

When you create a new query in Access 2016, you'll see two main panes split horizontally, both of which are initially blank. The top pane is there to contain the table or tables that will provide potential fields for the query. The bottom pane is a list of columns, each of which can contain one field that will display in the query's recordset when we execute it.

Adding data sources to a query

In the Query Design window, you can add data sources to your queries. A data source can be a table, or another query. Ultimately, every query still traces its origin to one or more tables.

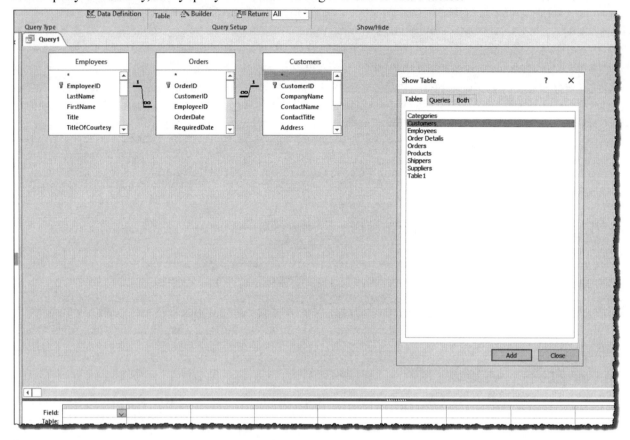

1. Click **Query Design**.

    Two blank windows appear, along with a popup from Access to choose tables and/or queries.

2. Double-click on each table or query you want to be part of the new query.

    A query is considered a data source just like a table in this case, even though every query can ultimately trace its origin to one or more tables.

    Your selections appear in the top pane.

3. When you're finished adding data sources, click **Close**.

When you add multiple data sources you'll see how they're related. In the above example, there are two relationships: The 1-to-many between Employees and Orders, and another 1-to-many between Customers and Orders.

About relationships

You should understand role of relationships when you choose the data sources for a query. If there are several tables that provide parts of the results for a query, those tables are typically related. If that's the case, you'll see a black line between them indicating that, just like what you see in the Relationships pane.

It's relatively uncommon, in fact, for a table that isn't related to at least one other table in the query to be present in a query. Think about it from a purely practical perspective: Let's say the query you're creating is going to be used in a report for your boss. An *unrelated* table in the query would mean *unrelated* data in the results, and if it's unrelated, your boss doesn't need to see it. Second, from a technical perspective the relationship provides the criteria for Access to join records when we execute the query. So, if there's no relationship, how does Access do the join? The short answer is that it still does, but the results probably aren't going to be something you'd want to present to your boss in that report.

The bottom line is that designing relationships correctly in the Relationships pane of Access is essential to creating queries that work and provide you with the answer to a business-related question.

Selecting query fields

Once you've added tables to the query, your next job is to choose which fields you want to be part of the query's results. There are two ways to add fields to the query's results.

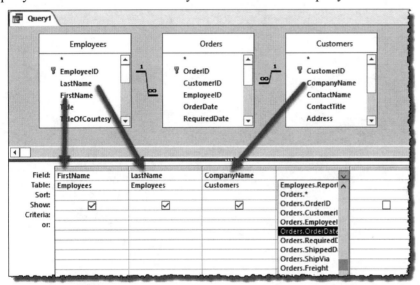

- In the top window, double-click on the field name displayed in any table.
    The field will be added to the right of any existing query columns.
- In the top window, click any cell in the **Field** row and select a field.
    When you're using this method, Access displays the field in *TableName.FieldName* format. If there's not enough room, you can always drag the column separator to the right so that Access will show you the entire field description.
- At any time during the process, click **Run** on the ribbon to see the returned recordset.

The recordset a query returns is determined by the relationship join type between the tables that are part of the query. In the above example, the query joining the Employees and Orders tables based on a match of the EmployeeID field value in each table. It is also returning a result from a join of the Customers and Orders tables based on a match of the CustomerID field value in each table. Notice that it isn't displaying an EmployeeID or CustomerID field in the results of this query, but that's how Access figures out what records to include in the results.

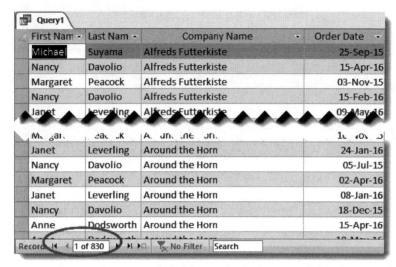

You can change the query definition to include more fields from each of the 3 tables, but it shouldn't affect the number of records you get. Access uses the same join criteria between tables regardless of which fields we request in this format.

Exercise: Creating a select query

Do This	How & Why
1. Open the sample database.	`SampleDB_BasicQueries.accdb`
2. Create a query.	To start, you'll just add a whole table to the query, but eventually you'll include multiple fields from multiple tables.
a) On the Create tab, click **Query Design**.	The Show Table window appears with a list of tables.
b) In the Show Table window, double-click **Customers**.	To add it to the Query window.
c) Close the Show table window.	
d) In the Customers table, double-click *****.	The asterisk represents all fields in the table.
e) On the Ribbon, click **Run**.	To display the results. The query shows all 91 records in the Customers table.
3. Add more tables to the query.	
a) On the ribbon, click **View**.	To return to Design View.
b) Show the Show Table window.	Click **Show Table** in the Query Setup group.

Do This	How & Why
c) Show the Orders table.	Double-click it.
d) Hide the Show Table window.	
e) Add all fields in the Orders table.	Double-click *****.
f) Click **Run**.	This time the query produces 830 records. This is because Access joins the two tables to produce one record in the query for each record in the Orders table.
g) Return to Query Design view.	
h) Add the Order Details and Products tables to your data sources.	In the Show Table window.
i) Add all fields in the Products table to the query.	Double-click *****.
4. Run the query.	Even if you didn't use any fields from the Order Details table, table relationships mean that adding the Products table fields made Order Details part of the SQL statement. You can click **View > SQL View** to verify this. There are now 2155 results, the number of records in the Order Details table.
5. Delete all existing query fields.	You didn't really want to so many fields to the query, so you'll delete the existing fields and make something more focused.
a) Enter Design View.	
b) In the lower pane, point to the gray bar at the top of the first column.	Until the cursor turns to a downward arrow.
c) Click the bar.	To select the column.
d) Press **Delete**.	
e) Delete the other columns.	Select each then press **Delete**.
6. Add relevant fields to the table.	Now you'll recreate the query using just the fields you actually need.
a) Add the **CompanyName** field from the Customers table.	In the top pane, double-click it.
b) Add **OrderDate** from the Orders table.	
c) From the Products table, add **ProductName** and **Discontinued**.	

Do This	How & Why
7. Run the revised query.	It still shows 2155 results, but now each record only shows the four fields you just chose.
8. Save the query.	
a) Click 💾 .	You're prompted for a query name.
b) Type `Customer Products Query`.	
c) Examine the Navigation pane.	The new query appears in the Queries node.

The query at the end of the exercise.

Company Name	Order Date	Product Name	Discontinue
QUICK-Stop	20-Sep-14	Chai	☐
Rattlesnake Canyon Grocery	30-Sep-14	Chai	☐
Lonesome Pine Restaurant	31-Oct-14	Chai	☐
Die Wandernde Kuh	08-Dec-14	Chai	☐
Pericles Comidas clásicas	15-Dec-14	Chai	☐
Chop-suey Chinese	03-Jan-15	Chai	☐
Queen Cozinha	07-Feb-15	Chai	☐
La maison d'Asie	14-Feb-15	Chai	☐
Princesa Isabel Vinhos	17-Apr-15	Chai	☐

Query criteria

If you simply add a list of fields to a query, Access returns all the records that match based on the join criteria from the relationship. Often though, you want to filter the results so that only certain records show up. Instead of all orders, what if you want to only see orders from last year? Or orders from customers in a certain country?

You can create one or more conditions using the Criteria line of the Fields window on the bottom in query design view. Remember your sample query above that returned 830 rows? Note the order date values in the rightmost column. Imagine only want orders where the Order Date is in the year 2015. You can add your criteria by simply typing them in the Criteria field. If you have to include the field name, you need to enclose it in square brackets, like *[FieldName]*.

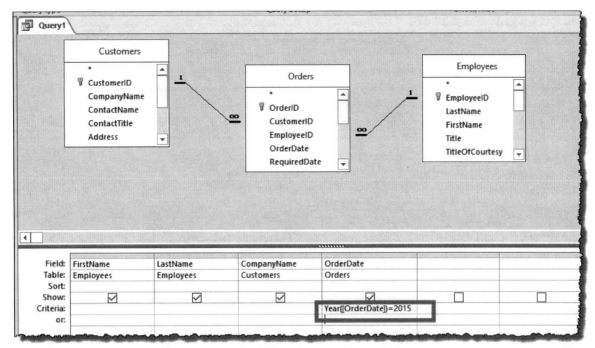

Now when you run the query you're going to get fewer records, just because not all the date values are in the requested range. In this example, the query with criteria set returns 391 records instead of over 800, because only values in 2015 are displayed.

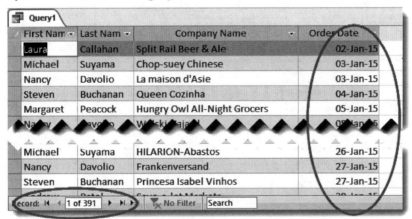

Remember, even when you only define criteria on a single field, a query returns records, not individual fields. Access returns an *entire record* to the query's recordset when the Criteria resolves to True for that field, and no record at all when the Criteria is False.

Adding multiple criteria conditions

You can use multiple criteria in the same query, but exactly how you do it depends on what kind of problem you're trying to solve. For example, you might want to find all orders that were placed by Canadian customers in 2015. This is called an *AND* condition, since the record must both have 2015 in its date field *and* Canada in its country field. Alternatively, you might want to find orders placed by customers in Canada or Mexico. This is called an *OR* condition. AND combinations are more restrictive than single criteria, since at least two separate criteria must be true. OR combinations are less restrictive, since any of multiple answers will give a true result.

- When you put criteria in the same row of separate fields (columns), Access adds an "AND" operator to join them.

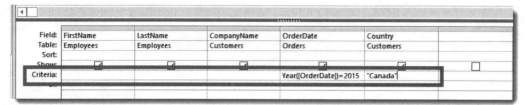

In this example, the query searches for year results of "2015" in OrderDate combined with "Canada" results in the Country field. Notice that since there's no function needed in the Country field, the value is just in double quotation marks. This is functionally equal to typing [Customers.Country]="Canada", which Access does behind the scenes.

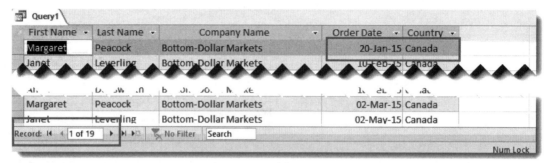

Since only results both in 2015 and Canada are returned, the results only show 19 records.

- When you add multiple conditions on separate rows, Access adds an "OR" between them.

In this case, Access will return both results from Canada, and results from Mexico.

- Even though the rows below the or: line are blank, you can continue to add additional "OR" criteria there and they'll function the same way as what you've seen so far.

Exercise: Adding criteria

To complete this exercise, you must first have created the Customer Products query.

Do This	How & Why
1. Open the Customer Products query.	Right-click it in the Navigation Pane and choose **Design View**.
2. Filter the query to include only discontinued products.	
a) On the Criteria line below the Discontinued field, type **Yes**.	Since it's a Boolean field, you can just add Yes or No.
b) Run the query.	There should be approximately 228 results, all with a check mark in the Discontinued field.
3. Add a second criteria to narrow the search further.	

Do This	How & Why
a) Return to Design View.	
b) On the Criteria line below the ProductName field, type in **Alice Mutton**.	To further restrict the results to products which are both discontinued and named Alice Mutton.
c) Run the query.	There are 37 results. All have "Alice Mutton" in the ProductName column.
4. Restrict the query to orders from 2015.	First, you'll add a field to show the year in which the discontinued product was ordered.
a) In the first blank field in the Field list, enter the expression `Year([OrderDate])`.	In Design View. This calculated field will display the year part of the order date only.
b) Right-click the field and click **Properties**, and then set the Caption property to `Order Year`.	
c) Run the query.	The results are the same as last time you ran it, but now each result has a four-digit year in the Year Ordered column.
d) In Design View, add a new criteria that shows orders only from 2015.	In the Criteria below the Year Ordered field, type `2015`.
e) Run the query.	Now it only shows orders for Alice Mutton that were made in 2015.
5. Save the query with a new name.	
a) Click **File > Save As > Save Object As > Save As**.	
b) Name the query `Discontinued Product Criteria Query`.	
c) Verify that the new query appears in the Queries node of the Navigation Pane, along with the previously created one.	

Parameter queries

Once you get used to using criteria you'll probably start thinking like "Sure, this time I want 2015 orders from Canadian customers. What if next time I want 2016 orders? Or orders from German customers?" Parameter queries are your solution.

With a Parameter query, you perform the design process the exact same way as before, until you get to the Criteria part. Instead, you format the criteria so that Access prompts the user running the query for a *parameter value*. Then Access performs the query, plugging the parameter in automatically, just as if you'd typed it there when you first designed the query. This gives queries that are reusable and dynamic.

For example, take that query that retrieves 2015 orders for Canadian customers, and make both of those values into parameters.

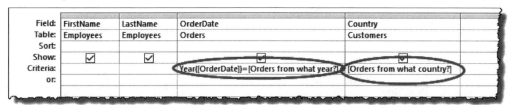

Notice the difference here between the first query where you hard-coded the values you wanted, and the new one with parameters. Instead of the value 2015, it has [Orders from what Year?], and instead of "Canada" it has [Orders from what Country?]. Don't be thrown off by the fact that the parameter has square brackets. Whenever Access sees a value in the [ ] that doesn't match an existing field name, it assumes you'll be supplying the value as a parameter at the time the query executes.

When you run this query to get 2014 orders from German customers, you'll see the following series of screens:

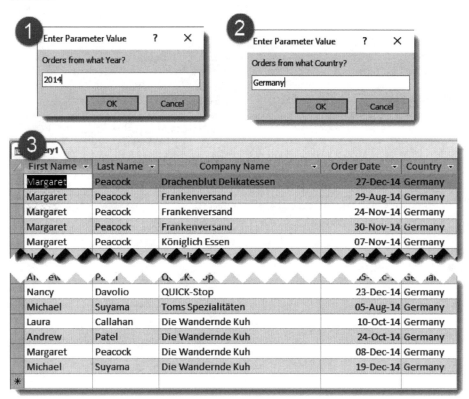

Adding data types to parameters

You can also restrict the information that's passed to the query by adding data types to the parameters. This will give a more helpful error message for the user if they don't enter the right type of data. As a best practice in query design, assign data types for numbers, currency, date/time values, or similar fields that shouldn't accept arbitrary text.

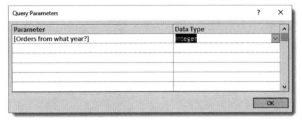

1. In Query Design view, click the **Parameters** button in the Show/Hide section of the ribbon.
2. Add the parameter name in the left column.
    Make sure the spelling matches the parameter in the Criteria row exactly.
3. Choose the required data type in the right column.
4. Click **OK**.

Exercise: Creating a Parameter query

The Discontinued Product Criteria Query is created.

Do This	How & Why
1. Open the Discontinued Product Criteria Query in Design View.	Right-click it and choose **Design View**.
2. Turn the hard-coded criteria values to parameters.	
a) Delete the existing ProductName criteria.	
b) In the ProductName Criteria field, type `[Product Name?]`.	Be sure to include the square brackets. The question mark isn't required, but it signals to the user that you're asking for information.
c) Replace the Year Ordered field criteria with `[Year Ordered?]`.	Delete the existing value and type it in.
3. Run the query.	
a) Click **Run**.	Before the query runs, you're asked for a product name.
b) In the Product Name? window, type `Alice Mutton`.	
c) Click **OK**.	You're now asked for a year.
d) Type `2015` and click **OK**.	The query runs, showing only Alice Mutton results from 2015.
4. Save the query as `Discontinued Product Parameter Query`.	Click **File > Save As > Save Object As > Save As.**

Totals queries

So far everything you've done with queries has involved single records. That is to say, there is one record in the recordset for every one record in query tables that match. In a *Totals query*, though, Access performs some function on a returned set of records, but instead of displaying the individual record values it only displays the *total* of a group of records.

This is a bit of a leap in complexity. It might be helpful to run your query as a normal Select query first to see the values that the Total query is acting on, then add in the Total functionality.

For example, let's say you want to see how many orders came from each country during 2015. You could start just by running a query that returns all 2015 orders. Once you're sure that's the right data, you can have Access aggregate it for you. To start the process, click the **Totals** button in the Show/Hide section of the ribbon. This adds a line labeled Total in the fields area. It also adds one very important rule to the query design:

In a Totals query, each field is either part of a group **or** *displays the result of an aggregate function.*

Field:	Country	OrderID
Table:	Customers	Orders
Total:	Group By	Count
Sort:		
Show:	✓	✓

Access enforces this requirement by providing only those choices in the Total drop-down box. You either choose "Group By" to make the field part of the grouping, or one of the aggregate functions (Sum, Average, Count, etc.). You can have as many aggregate fields displayed as you want, but there must be at least one Group By field in the query. (You could leave all the fields set to Group By, but that defeats the purpose of doing a Totals query since you'll just get the same thing you would have with a normal Select query).

Practically speaking, Totals queries generally involve fewer fields than normal select queries, just because that's the nature of the information you're looking for. If you're grouping on Last Name, City, *and* Order Date to show a count of orders, for example, Access will return a record for *each* unique combination of Last Name, City and Order Date. This may or may not be helpful. If you eliminate Last Name and City from this query, though, you'll get a count of orders for each unique Order Date *only*. Keep in mind that you are creating one record in the recordset for *each* unique set of fields marked Group By in the Total row. Too many Group fields generally means that the results are going to be too unfocused to be useful in business decision making.

Creating totals queries

Say you want to find out how many orders came from each country in 2015. Here's the query as a basic select:

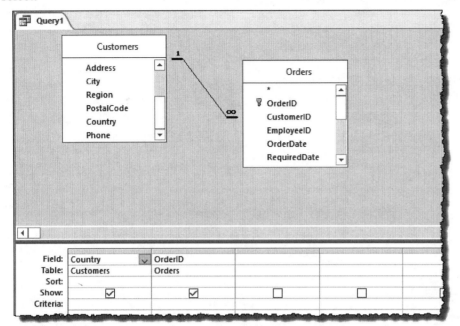

This query produces one record in the query recordset for each Order in the Orders table, since Orders is on the many side of the 1-to-many relationship. To get a count of the number of orders from each country, you could use a Total query.

1. Click **Totals** in the Show/Hide group of the Ribbon.
2. Set the Totals row for each field in the query.
   - At least one field must be left as **Group By**.
   - For one or more fields, choose an aggregate function.
     In this example, you'll group by the Country field, and choose **Count** for OrderID.

In the query results, Access will automatically name the total field to give users a hint as to what kind of data they're looking at. In this example, the query's results will have two fields: Country, and CountOfOrderID.

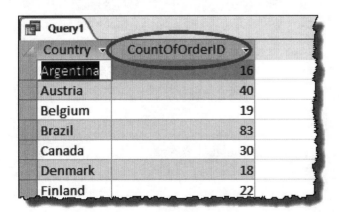

Exercise: Creating a Totals query

Do This	How & Why
1. Begin a new query.	
a) Open Design View.	Click **Query Design**.
b) Add the **Customers**, **Orders**, **Order Details**, **Products**, and **Categories** tables.	From the Show Table window.
c) Click **Close**.	In the Show Table window.
d) Arrange the tables in the window so that the relationships are clear to you.	
2. Create a Select query.	To get an idea of what the Totals query data should look like, you'll create a Select query first.
a) Add **CompanyName** from the Customers table.	Double-click it.
b) Add **OrderID** from Order Details.	
c) In the next blank field, type `Line Item Total: [Order Details].[UnitPrice]*[Quantity]`	This calculated field shows the total price of each entry.
d) In the Sort cell of the OrderID field, choose **Ascending**.	To sort by the Order ID value.
e) Run the query.	There should be multiple Line Item Total results for some orders, representing different categories.
f) Find OrderID 10267.	There are three entries with the same OrderID since they represent separate product categories.
	Query1 — Company Name / Order I / Line Item To: Wartian Herkku 10266 $364.80; Frankenversand 10267 $216.00; Frankenversand 10267 $735.00; Frankenversand 10267 $3,080.00; GROSELLA-Restaurante 10268 $111.20
	The three records should add up to $4031.
3. Turn the Select query into a Totals query.	You want to show an order total based on the sum of the line items for each order.
a) In Query Design view, click **Totals**.	In the Show/Hide group of the Ribbon. A Totals row appears in the bottom pane.

Do This	How & Why
b) In the Total cell of the Line Item Total field, choose **Sum**.	Leave **Group By** in the other Total fields.
c) Run the query.	There is now only one line for each combination of company name and Order ID.
d) Examine Order ID 10267.	The total is $4031, as expected.
4. Save the query as **Customer Order Totals Query**.	

Crosstab queries

There are cases where you'd like to aggregate data based on two criteria. You could use the Totals query, but the results might not be easily readable. This is where a *Crosstab query* comes in. This special type of Select query returns one aggregate based on two criteria in easy-to-read spreadsheet-style format that Excel users will find particularly familiar.

Imagine you want to find out how many orders you received from a particular country in a particular month. As a Totals query, you could design it this way:

(You've created your own custom expression for the field labeled OrderMonth. For example, when the order was placed in June of 2015 it will say 6/2015). This query produces one record for each unique combination of country and month, and shows how many orders were placed.

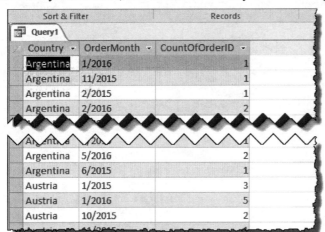

The data is accurate, but not very readable. You have to scroll through the entire list to see how many orders were placed in a particular month, and there's no easy way to compare one month or one country to another. So, you'll redesign this as a Crosstab query.

Creating crosstab queries

A crosstab query is like a spreadsheet. You can create one by assigning which field corresponds to which "spreadsheet" element.

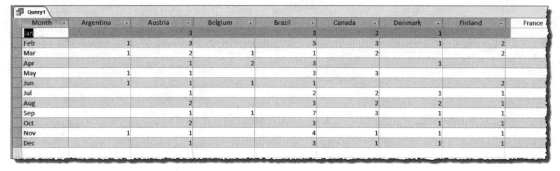

1. In Design View, click **Crosstab** in the Query Type group.
2. Set a Crosstab value for each field.
   - Choose one **Column heading**.
   - Choose at least one **Row heading**.
   - Choose one **Value** for an aggregate value.
   - Set any other fields to **(not shown)**.

In the above example, the Country field is the Column heading, the Month field is the Row heading, and the Value is the aggregate number of orders from that country in that month. There's also an expression field that's used to sort the months based on numeric value, but it's not shown.

Exercise: Creating a crosstab query

Do This	How & Why
1. Open **Customer Order Totals Query** in Design View.	
2. Add the **CategoryName** field from the Categories table to the query.	In our Crosstab query, we want to see what categories our customers spend the most money in. If you want to reposition any fields in the query, select the field column to highlight it, then drag it to a new location.
3. On the Ribbon, click **Crosstab**.	In the Query Type section. The Crosstab row appears.
4. Assign fields to Crosstab values.	To make the crosstab query work, now you need to assign fields as column heading, row heading, and value.
a) In the Crosstab row, set CompanyName as **Row Heading**.	In general, it's better to set the field with more possible entries as a row heading.
b) Set CategoryName as **Column Heading**.	
c) Set Line Item Total as **Value**.	
d) Set OrderID as **(not shown)**.	You don't need to include this in the query results.
5. Run the query.	Technically it's not even a Line Item Total now, but a complete grand total. You should have multiple CompanyName values for some customers, with the Line Item total value shown under its category name.

Do This	How & Why
6. In Design View, change the OrderID Crosstab cell to **Row Heading**.	Access allows multiple Row Heading fields in a Crosstab query.
7. Save the query as `Customer Order Total Crosstab Query`.	
8. Edit the query.	You'll use the query to demonstrate total customer spending by category.
a) In Design View, delete the **OrderID** field from the field list.	Select the field and press **Delete**.
b) Run the query again.	Since you eliminated OrderID as a field to group on, the query results now show a total for each individual combination of CompanyName and CategoryName only. Each customer now only appears once, and the crosstab value shows a grand total of all spending for a category.
9. Close the query without saving it.	You want to retain the OrderID field for later.

Basic Action query types

Action queries perform an action on data, and where they shine is that they let you perform the action any time, on demand. You can use a basic action query to perform one of four primary tasks.

- Create a new table
- Add records to an existing table
- Update one or more records in a table
- Delete records from a table, as long as the table's relationships allow it.

In this section, you'll explore the different types of available action queries and map them to the common actions you might want to perform on your data.

Make Table queries

Just like the name says, a *Make Table query* will make a new table from existing data using the criteria you specify. For a simple example of a Make Table query, imagine a query that finds all Canadian orders from 2015. The difference is that instead of just displaying them onscreen, it uses them to create a whole new table. In this example, the data comes from a table in the same database, but it's also effective for creating a snapshot of data from an external source. The design principle remains the same in any case.

Running the query will produce a pop-up from Access alerting you to the fact that you're creating a table, and telling you how many records you're adding to it. If the table already exists, you'll see another pop-up warning you that the table will be dropped and then re-created if you run the query. It's all good information to be alerted to, especially if you're used to running select queries where we're not changing anything about the data. Action queries always perform an action on data, so it's good that Access reminds you of that fact before you do something that's a potential mistake.

There is no connection between the original table(s) that the data came from and the new table you create *after you run the query*. In our example, if you entered new orders dated 2015 for Canadian customers after running the Make Table query, those new orders would *not* be automatically reflected in the query results.

Creating Make Table queries

Like other action queries, a Make Table query starts off much like a Select query. The difference is that it takes actions based on what it finds, instead of just displaying it. For this example, let's say you want to eventually make a table out of 2015 order information for your Canadian customers.

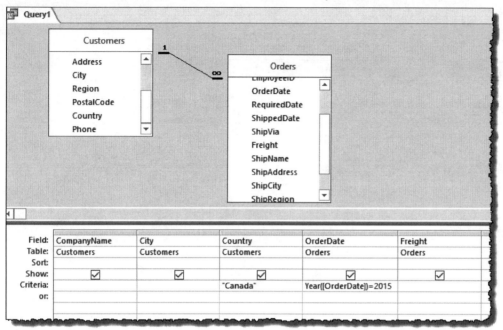

1. Design the data you want as a normal Select query.
2. In the Query Type group, click **Make Table**.
3. Choose a name for the new table.
4. Click **OK**.

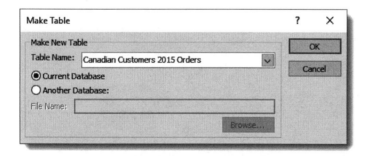

Exercise: Creating a Make Table Query

In this exercise, you will create a new table containing mailing list information for your suppliers.

Do This	How & Why
1. Create a Select query showing mailing list information.	You can use a Select query to find all the information you need.
a) Create a new Query in Design View.	
b) Add the **Suppliers** table to the query's data sources.	Close the **Show Table** window when you're done.
c) Add **ContactName** to the query.	
d) Add all other fields you'd expect to see on a mailing address.	**Address**, **City**, **Region**, **PostalCode**, and **Country**.
e) In the Sort cell under the **Country** field, choose **Ascending**.	
f) Run the query to test it.	It produces 29 results, sorted by country.
2. Change the Select query to a Make Table query.	
a) Enter Design View	
b) In the Query Type group, click **Make Table**.	The **Make Table** window appears.
c) In the Table Name field, type `Mailing List`.	If you wanted you could even create the table in a different database.
d) Click **OK**.	
3. Run the new query.	
a) Click **Run**.	Access warns you that you're about to paste 29 rows into a new table.
b) Click **Yes**.	The Mailing List table now appears in the Objects list in the Navigation Pane.
c) Open the Mailing List table.	Unlike a Select query, this new table won't be affected if the Suppliers database is altered later. It holds the same information that the original Select query generated.
4. Save the new query as **Mailing List Make Table Query**.	
5. Close all open objects.	Leave the database open.

Append queries

An Append query is a close cousin of the Make Table query. An Append query adds records to an existing table. As with other action query types, it's best to start here with a select query, make sure the data is accurate, then convert to an Append query.

Let's say you already created a new table showing order information for your Canadian customers in 2015, and the boss says the format is right but the table should include all of North America. To fix this, you can create a query that selects order information for USA and Mexican customers, and then make it into an Append query that will add the records to the existing table.

Creating Append queries

An Append query has two major differences from a Make Table query. The most obvious is that it adds records to those that already exist. The other is that you need to work within the structure of an existing table rather than creating a new one. That means you need to make sure that every field in the query *maps* to a field in the destination table.

1. Design the data you want as a normal Select query.

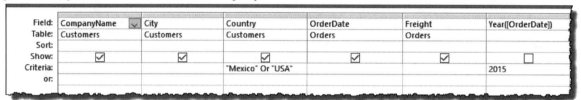

2. In the Query Type group, click **Append**.
3. In the Append window, choose an existing destination table and click **OK**.

    Access will attempt to map fields in the query to fields in the table by matching field names.

4. If any fields don't automatically map properly, choose a destination field in the **Append to** cell.

    If a field isn't supposed to map, for example one just used as a filter, don't map it at all.

Just like when you run a Make Table query, when you run an Append query Access warns you that you're going to be adding records. If the purpose of the table changed, as it did in this case, be sure to rename it so that users know what to expect. This example table should probably be renamed from Canadian Customers 2015 Orders to North American Customers 2015 Orders.

Append query errors

If errors occur while running an Append query, there are several common causes. You'll need to scrub the data to conform to the new rules before you can run the query successfully. Here are some common problems:

Data type mismatch — You cannot, for example, add text data to a Date/Time field.

Validation rule violation — Validation rules from the original table must be observed when appending data, including not only custom validation rules but required fields.

Key violation — Primary key and foreign key rules from the original table must be observed. Attempting to add a duplicate primary key value, or a foreign key value that doesn't match an existing primary key, will case the Append query to fail.

Exercise: Creating an Append query

To complete this exercise, the Mailing List table must already exist.

In this exercise, you'll create an Append query that adds new records to the Mailing List table.

Do This	How & Why
1. Create a Select query that displays address information for your employee records.	One problem with adding employee records to your existing mailing list is that Employees has separate fields for first and last names.
a) Create a new Query in Design View.	
b) Add the **Employees** table to the query's data sources.	Close the **Show Table** window when you're done.
c) Add the **LastName** field to the query.	Don't add FirstName. You'll get to that later.
d) Add all other fields you'd expect to see on a mailing address.	**Address**, **City**, **Region**, **PostalCode**, and **Country**.
e) Edit the LastName Field row to read `[FirstName] & " " & [LastName]`.	Access will automatically name this new calculated field Expr1. You needn't be concerned about the field name here, since you'll eventually be putting this data into an existing field in an existing table.
2. Run the query.	The query returns 9 results, and the Expr1 field shows both first and last name for each Employee.
3. Change the query to an Append query.	You'll have the query append its results to the Mailing list table.
a) Return to Query Design view.	

Do This	How & Why
b) In the Query Type group, click **Append**.	The Append window appears.
c) From the Table name list, select **Mailing List**.	Since you're appending instead of creating, you need to select an existing table.
d) Click **OK**.	An Append to row appears in the bottom pane. The last five fields map automatically to those in the existing table, but Expr1 does not.
e) In the Append to cell below Expr1, choose **ContactName**.	
4. Test the new query.	
a) Click **Run**.	Access warns you that you are about to append rows to an existing table.
b) Click **Yes**.	
c) Open the Mailing List table.	It contains the new employee entries in addition to its previous contents.
5. Save the query as `Mailing List Append Query`.	
6. Close all open objects.	

Update queries

An Update query changes values for one or more fields in every record that matches the query criteria. While it is technically possible to update all records in a table, more often Update queries are used to change a certain subset of records based on some condition. If your job is to update the price of all products in a certain product category, an update query is the ideal way to accomplish this.

Preparing update queries

Like with other action queries, you should start with a Select query to make sure it returns the right records before you turn it into an Update query. In fact, it's a good idea to be even more careful with an Update query than an Append, because it will make changes that will be hard to undo. For example, to create a price update query you would proceed as follows.

1. Create a Select query with the fields you want.

Field:	CategoryName	ProductName	UnitPrice
Table:	Categories	Products	Products
Sort:			
Show:	☑	☑	☑
Criteria:	[Product Category?]		
or:			

 Note: There's a method to the apparent madness here in parameterizing the select query in this example. Let's say that company policy is to update all the products in a category at the same time. In designing the query this way, you'll be able to have the query prompt for a category (And eventually, how much you want to change the pricing) when you switch it to an Update query.

2. Run the Select query to evaluate and refine the results.

   In this case, you should run it multiple times, plugging in the appropriate CategoryName at each prompt. All you're trying to do at this point is to make sure that the final Update query will update the records you want without altering any others. If you're not sure that the update formula is correct, you can just add it as its own field while this is still a select query, then compare the values of the original and the updated field.

3. Enter the updated value you want to insert as a new calculated field.

   Testing it in a Select query lets you make sure the new values are right before you apply them permanently.

CategoryName	ProductName	UnitPrice	New Price: [UnitPrice]*(1+[Price Change Pct?]/100)	
Categories	Products	Products		
☑	☑	☑	☑	
[Product Category?]				

In this case, a parameter in the calculated field lets you try different percentages.

4. Test the Select query with new results.

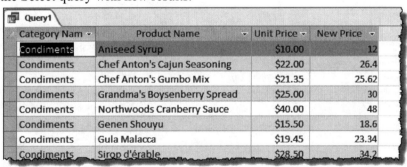

Now you can see the original value and new value side by side, without affecting the original table.

Creating update queries

Once you have a tested and polished Select query, you can turn it into an Update query.

1. In Query Design View, click **Update** on the ribbon.

    The Update to row appears in the lower pane.

2. Fill out the **Update to** cell of the field you want to update.

    In this example, you can move your expression field there.

    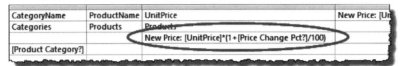

3. Delete the test field you created.

Exercise: Creating an Update query

To complete this exercise, the Mailing List table must already exist and contain both supplier and employee data.

An arcane postal service regulation has been discovered that requires the Country field in all mailing labels to read "United States of America" instead of "USA". You'll use an Update Query to make this change to all Mailing List table records.

Do This	How & Why
1. Create a Select query.	First you need to make sure you're only showing addresses in the US.
a) Create a new Query in Design View.	
b) Add the **Mailing List** table to your data sources.	
c) Add * to the query fields.	To display all fields in Mailing List as part of the query.
d) Add the **Country** field.	You're already showing all fields, but you want to add the Country field separately so you can add Criteria to it.
e) Clear the **Show** box in the Country column.	To keep the Country field from showing twice in the results.
f) In the Criteria cell under the Country field, enter **USA**.	
2. Run the query.	It shows 9 values, all with "USA" as the Country value.
3. Change the query to an update query.	Now that you know it works as a Select query, it's safe to convert it.
a) Enter Design View.	

Access 2016 Relational Database Design

Do This	How & Why
b) In the Query Type group, click **Update**.	The Sort and Show rows are hidden, but the Update to row appears.
c) In the Update to field under Country, enter `United States of America`.	
d) Delete the **Mailing List.*** field.	You're not updating any other fields, so they don't need to be part of the Update query.

Field:	Country
Table:	Mailing List
Update To:	"United States of America"
Criteria:	"USA"
or:	

4. Test the finished query.

   a) Click **Run**. — Access asks whether you want to update nine rows.

   b) Click **Yes**. — To run the query.

   c) Open the Mailing List table. — All "USA" mailing addresses are changed to "United States of America." Other countries aren't affected.

5. Save the query as `Update Mailing List Query`.

6. Close all open objects.

Delete queries

The Delete query follows the same pattern as the other action queries: you should design it as a select query, run the query to check the accuracy of your syntax, and then switch to a Delete query.

There's one important detail here, though.

Instead of acting on values like the Update query, the Delete query deletes entire rows. It can only do that successfully though, if the relationships the table is involved in allow it. For example, let's say Customers and Orders are related, and the relationship rules state that for every CustomerID in the Orders table (The many side of the 1-to-many relationship), there must be a matching CustomerID in the Customers table (The "one" side of the relationship).

Note: You can discover the rules about existing relationships using the Relationships window. Double-click on the black line between two tables to open the Edit Relationships window.

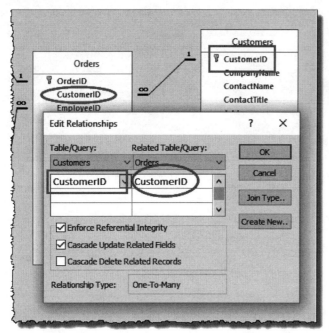

Notice that in this relationship, referential integrity is enforced, but that the Cascade Delete Related Fields box is unchecked. This means Access will *disallow* the deletion of any rows from the Customers table where a matching CustomerID value exists in the Orders table. There's a very good reason for this: you want to avoid *orphaned rows*. If there's no CustomerID to match to, the Order information is *orphaned*, meaning that it's not attached to a certain customer. Obviously, this is a problem Before you start designing Delete queries, check all the relationships a table is part of.

Many developers also consider Delete queries to be a security risk, since they make it easy to delete important data by mistake. Even though Access will show you the usual prompt you see for action queries, warning you that you're about to delete records, some users will plow through this with nary a second thought. Delete query results are also not undoable. If you just want to change the status of a record, consider an alternative that keeps the records available just in case someone (not you of course) deletes something they shouldn't have.

- *A status field*. Having an Active Customer field of data type Yes/No in a Customers table makes it easy to only see active customers, just by designing a query with that criteria. Instead of deleting a customer when they stop ordering, just switch their status to inactive.

- *A macro*. You can create a macro that runs multiple action queries. In this case, you could do an Append Query that adds inactive customer information to an InactiveCustomers table, and then run a Delete Query that deletes the same customers from the original table.

Exercise: Creating a delete query

To complete this exercise, the Mailing List table must already exist and contain both client and employee data. Due to new import regulations, you have to discontinue your Japanese suppliers. You'll use a Delete query to remove them from the mailing list.

Do This	How & Why
1. Create a Select query to find all Japanese addresses in the mailing list. a) Create a new Query in Design View.	

Do This	How & Why
b) Add the **Mailing List** table to your data sources.	
c) Add * to the query fields.	To display all fields in Mailing List as part of the query.
d) Add the **Country** field.	
e) Clear the **Show** box in the Country column.	To keep the Country field from showing twice in the results.
f) In the Criteria cell under the Country field, enter **Japan**.	
2. Run the query.	It shows two results, both in Japan.
3. Change the query to a Delete query.	
a) Enter Query Design View.	
b) In the Query Type group, click **Delete**.	
	The Sort and Show rows are hidden, and the Delete row appears. You can leave the Delete and Criteria rows as they are.
4. Test the query.	
a) Click **Run**.	A popup asks if you really want to delete two rows.
b) Click **Yes**.	To run the query.
c) Open the **Mailing List** table.	If you want to sort the country values to make sure there are no Japanese addresses, right-click in the **Country** column and choose **Sort A to Z**. It now has no Japanese addresses.
5. Save the query as `Mailing List Delete Query`.	
6. Close all open objects.	
7. Close the database.	

Assessment: Creating basic queries

1. What query type has an output similar to that of a spreadsheet? Choose the best response.
   - Append
   - Crosstab
   - Parameter
   - Totals

2. You're reviewing a query that displays order details. Below the Category field, there are two Criteria on two separate rows: "Beverages" and "Produce." What results will the query show? Choose the best response.
   - All orders with items in both the Beverages and Produce categories
   - All orders with items in either the Beverages or Produce categories
   - All orders with Beverages but no Produce, or Produce but no Beverages
   - No orders at all

3. It's often best practice to add data types to parameters, but it depends on the field type. True or false?
   - True
   - False

4. Which kind of query might not work because of table relationship rules? Choose the best response.
   - Append
   - Delete
   - Make Table
   - Update

Module B: Modifying queries

Initial query design is most often just the start. In this module, you'll look at all the ways you can modify existing queries. For simplicity, the following examples will use Select queries, but the same concepts would apply to Action queries as well.

You will learn:

- How to rename query fields
- How to organize query fields
- How to sort query results
- About query field formatting

Changing field names and the field list

After designing a query, we may need to add, delete or rename fields, and manipulate the way the information is displayed. While Access will present recordsets in a sort order it determines, that's often not sufficient so you need to add that, too. You may also want to hide certain fields from the recordset view even if you've included them, for example to enforce a Criteria condition. It's fairly simple to do any of these in Query Design view, without otherwise affecting the functioning of the query.

Renaming query fields

Renaming fields in a table isn't always practical or advised. There may be other objects (like SQL code) that depend on field names remaining static, but you can always display a field name of your choice in a query by simply adding the new name to the field itself.

When the query result field comes from a table, Access automatically uses the Caption value from the table field, or just the actual field name if Caption isn't supplied. This will often be enough to give you a user-friendly field name in the query results. If you want to have your own field name in the query only that doesn't affect the table, each field's property sheet contains a Caption property you can set independently.

More often the need to rename a field will come into play with calculated fields, when you want to present a value that's the result of some function you performed on the actual table data. If you don't rename the field, Access will use its default of Expr1, and increment that for successive calculated fields (Expr2, Expr3, etc.) This isn't very informative for the user, so you can substitute our own labels. To be clear, a label is really all this is. You're not technically "renaming the field" from the table, you're putting a label on the field that shows in the query results.

You can place a label on your choice in two ways.

- Set the Caption property for the field.

    a) Select the field.

    b) Click **Property Sheet** in the Show/Hide group of the Ribbon.

    c) Enter a label value in the **Caption** field.

- When entering a calculated field, begin it by typing the field name you want, followed by a colon.

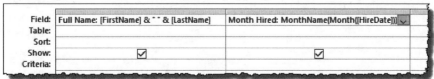

Adding, removing, and hiding fields

Adding a field to a query is as simple as finding the right-most blank column in the field window and choosing a field name from the drop-down or creating an expression for a calculated field. You can usually add a field to a query with little concern about how it affects existing forms or reports that use the query. At worst, you'll end up with an extra field that the form or report or query doesn't use. Similarly, changing the order of a query's fields doesn't really affect much other than the layout of its results.

Actually deleting query fields is another matter. This is where you have to consider the impact the deletion will have on forms, reports or other queries that use this query. From a technical perspective, a form that uses the query as a data source will still run but will show the cryptic value `#Name?` in form fields that are missing in the underlying data source. From a business perspective, you've deleted information that's been deemed necessary. So just be careful: just because you *can* do it doesn't mean you should.

- To select a query for moving or deleting, click the thin gray line directly above the Field row. When it's selected, the whole column will be highlighted.

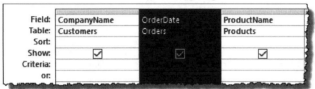

- To delete a field, select it and press **Delete**.
- To move a field, select it then drag it by the top bar to the line between any two other fields.
- To hide a field from query results without deleting it, clear the **Show** box under the field.

Exercise: Modifying a query

Do This	How & Why
1. Open the `SampleDB_ModifyingQueriesStart` database.	
2. Create a query to show product and order information.	First, you'll create a basic query, then you can modify it.
a) Create a new query in Design View.	
b) Add the **Orders**, **Order Details**, and **Products** tables to your data sources.	Close the Show Table window afterward.
c) From the Orders table, add **OrderID**, **EmployeeID**, and **OrderDate**.	Double-click on each.
d) From the Order Details table, add **OrderID** and **Quantity**.	
e) From the Products table, add **ProductName**.	
3. Run the query.	Every record has two identical OrderID columns, one from Orders and one from Order Details.

Do This	How & Why
4. Rename a field label.	By default, the field captions are inherited from the tables you used as data sources, but you can still change them here.
a) Enter Design View.	
b) Select the **EmployeeID** field.	
c) In the Show/Hide group, click **Property Sheet**.	The Property Sheet pane opens.
d) In the Caption field, type `Salesperson`.	On the General tab.
e) Close the Property Sheet.	
f) Run the query.	The caption is now shown in the header row.
5. Delete a field.	There are two Order ID fields, so you'll delete one of them.
a) Enter Design View.	
b) Select the **OrderID** field from the Order Details table.	Point to the thin gray bar above the field name.
c) Press **Delete**.	To delete the field from the query.
6. Add two new fields to the query.	You'll add each field a different way.
a) In the Products table, double-click **UnitsInStock**.	In the top pane.
b) Click and hold the **ReorderLevel** field in the Products table.	You'll insert this field in between two existing fields.
c) Drag the field on top of the **Quantity** field in the query.	The ReorderLevel field is inserted to the left of the Quantity field.
d) Test the query.	It shows the new fields you've added, and only one Order ID field.
7. Save the query as `Modified Products Query`.	

Do This	How & Why
8. Close all open objects.	

Modified Products Query						
Order ID	Salesperson	Order Date	Reorder Leve	Quantity	Product Name	Units In Stoc
10285	Davolio, Nancy	20-Sep-14	10	45	Chai	39
10294	Peacock, Margaret	30-Sep-14	10	18	Chai	39
10317	Suyama, Michael	31-Oct-14	10	20	Chai	39
10348	Peacock, Margaret	08-Dec-14	10	15	Chai	39
10354	Callahan, Laura	15-Dec-14	10	12	Chai	39
10370	Suyama, Michael	03-Jan-15	10	15	Chai	39
10406	Rey, Robert	07-Feb-15	10	10	Chai	39
10413	Leverling, Janet	14-Feb-15	10	24	Chai	39
10477	Buchanan, Steven	17-Apr-15	10	15	Chai	39
10522	Peacock, Margaret	31-May-15	10	40	Chai	39
10526	Peacock, Margaret	05-Jun-15	10	8	Chai	39
10576	Leverling, Janet	24-Jul-15	10	10	Chai	39
10590	Peacock, Margaret	07-Aug-15	10	20	Chai	39
10609	Rey, Robert	24-Aug-15	10	3	Chai	39

Sorting query results

Access applies a default sort order to query results, but it might not make such intuitive sense when you first look at it. This is especially the case if you've got many tables joined together that are supplying the query results. Internally, Access uses table indexes to efficiently select or eliminate ranges of records to satisfy the query criteria. Your query results are not always created in the order you specify the tables or even the fields.

If the default sort isn't good for your purposes, you can sort a query's results either by single or multiple fields. Note that sorts can be computationally expensive, especially with large databases. When performance might be an issue, avoid sorting at all unless it's actually necessary for the form, report, or query where you're using the results.

- To sort by a single field, click the drop-down arrow in the **Sort** row for that field.
  - Choose **Ascending** to sort lowest to highest for numbers, earliest to latest for dates, or A to Z for text.
  - Choose **Descending** to sort the opposite direction.
- To sort by multiple fields, you need to arrange query fields matching the order you wish to sort in.
    When there are multiple sorting fields, Access will perform the first (primary) sort field on all records. It will only perform the secondary search on records where the primary field is identical, and so on.

a) Choose a sort direction for each field you wish to sort by.

b) Move the *primary* sort field to the left of all other sort fields.
   For example, if LastName is the primary sort, all results will be sorted by last name.

c) Move the *secondary* sort field to the right of the primary sort field.
   For example, if HireDate is the secondary field, records will only be sorted by hire date if their last names are identical.

d) Repeat the process for each further sort field.

Results of the above search

First Name	Last Name	Hire Date
James	Buchanan	18-Jan-17
Steven	Buchanan	17-Oct-13
Laura	Callahan	05-Mar-11
Nancy	Davolio	01-May-13
Anne	Dodsworth	15-Nov-14
Janet	Leverling	01-Apr-15
Andrew	Patel	14-Aug-07

Exercise: Sorting a query

To complete this exercise, Modified Products Query must be created.

Do This	How & Why
1. Open **Modified Products Query** in Design View.	
2. Add a single sort field.	
a) Under the OrderDate field, click the **Sort** field and choose **Descending**.	
b) Run the query.	The query shows the same results as before, but they're all sorted from newest to oldest. Records with the same order date still use the default Access sort.
3. Add a secondary sort field.	When the order date is the same, you want to show larger quantities first.
a) Return to Design View.	
b) Apply a **Descending** sort to the Quantity field.	Click the **Sort** field then choose **Descending**.
c) Run the query.	The query is still sorted by date, but within each day's results records are sorted by quantity, highest to lowest.
4. Change the sort order.	On second thought, you'd rather sort by quantity first, and by order date second. To do so, you need to reorder the query fields.
a) In Design View, select the **Quantity** column.	Click the gray bar at the top.
b) Drag the field to the left of the OrderDate field.	Even if you drop it on top of OrderDate, it will end up on the left.

Access 2016 Relational Database Design

Do This	How & Why
c) Run the query.	Now the largest quantities are shown first, and records are only sorted by date when the quantities are identical.
5. Save the query as `Modified Products With Sort Query`.	Click **File** > **Save As** > **Save Object As** > **Save As**.
6. Close all open objects.	

Modified Products Query

Order ID	Salesperson	Quantity	Order Date	Reorder Level	Product Name	Units In Stock
11072	Peacock, Margaret	130	04-Jun-16	30	Wimmers gute Semm	22
10764	Suyama, Michael	130	03-Jan-16	5	Chartreuse verte	69
10894	Davolio, Nancy	120	20-Mar-16	25	Rhönbräu Klosterbie	125
10776	Davolio, Nancy	120	15-Jan-16	10	Manjimup Dried App	20
10711	Buchanan, Steven	120	21-Nov-15	0	Perth Pasties	0
10678	Rey, Robert	120	24-Oct-15	10	Jack's New England C	85
10595	Patel, Andrew	120	10-Aug-15	25	Sirop d'érable	113
10515	Patel, Andrew	120	24-May-15	30	Schoggi Schokolade	49
10451	Peacock, Margaret	120	22-Mar-15	20	Pâté chinois	115

Query field formatting

Often, you'll probably want to format the appearance of certain fields, such as choosing the display format of a date, or whether a numerical value should be shown as currency or percentage. While you can format a field in its originating table, you might not want to.

One reason is philosophical. Tables are the raw storage location for your data, so it's more important to make sure that their data is normalized (stored in a maintainable and efficient way) than it is to worry about how it looks. By this reasoning, it's better to leave formatting to the forms, reports, and queries that present table data to users. The other reason is more practical. The raw data in a table might be used in many end locations, each with different needs. This means it makes more sense to apply formatting later in the process where you can better guess how the end result should look. Queries are a popular place to apply formatting for this reason, even when the query itself might become the data source for a form, a report, or even another query.

Formatting query fields

Exactly how you can format a query field depends on what kind of data it holds, but usually the easiest way to do it is from the Property Sheet pane. To open it, either click **Property Sheet** on the ribbon, or right-click the field and choose **Properties**.

- To format a Date field, click **Format** and choose from any of the available date formats.

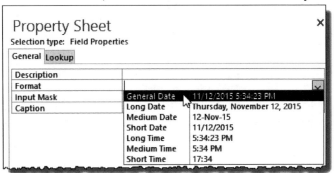

In addition to the full date and time format, you can choose various formats for just the date, and just the time.

- To format a number field, click **Format** to change the numerical formatting, or click **Decimal places** to change how many decimal places to display in the result.

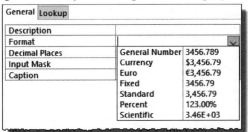

- Text fields don't offer any formatting options from the drop-down list. Instead, you can apply one of the many string functions available in *Visual Basic for Applications (VBA)*. To do so, apply the string in the Field cell itself, rather than in the Properties Sheet pane.

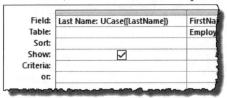

For example, if you want to display employee last names in upper case, you would enter the expression `Last Name: UCase([LastName])`.

Common string functions

VBA includes a lot of string functions you can use for formatting. The following common examples use [FieldName] as a placeholder for the actual field name you'd fill in.

- `UCase([FieldName])`: Returns the whole string as upper case letters.
  - Example: `UCase("AcCeSS")` returns the value "ACCESS"
- `LCase([FieldName])`: The opposite of upper case.
  - `LCase("AcCeSS")` returns the value "access"
- `Left([FieldName],#)` or `Right([FieldName],#)`: Returns some number of characters from the original string, the exact number being designated by the # placeholder. Left returns that number of characters from the beginning of the string, while Right returns that number from the end.
  - `Left("Access",3)` returns the value "Acc"
  - `Right("Access",4)` returns the value "cess"
- `Trim([FieldName])`: Removes any leading or trailing spaces and returns the new string without spaces.
  - `Trim(" there is a lot of space here ")` returns the string "there is a lot of space here"
- `Replace([FieldName],ValueToRemove,ValueToInsert)`: Replaces *ValueToRemove* with *ValueToInsert* every place it appears in [FieldName].
  - `Replace("elephant","e","X")` returns the value "XlXphant".

Exercise: Formatting a query

Do This	How & Why
1. Open **Modified Products With Sort Query** in Design view.	
2. Format a text field using a string function.	Management has decided that product names need to be shortened to a standard length. You will apply a string function to accomplish this.
a) In the query field list, select the **ProductName** field cell.	
b) Type `Left([ProductName],10)`.	This will display the first ten characters of the product name.
c) In the Show/Hide group of the ribbon, click **Property Sheet**.	You'll change the caption to reflect that it's a truncated value.
d) Click the **ProductName** field again.	If necessary.

Do This	How & Why
e) In the Caption field, type **Short Product Name**.	
f) Run the query.	The caption is changed and the product names cut off after ten characters.
3. Format the Order Date field using a standard date format.	
a) Return to Query Design View.	
b) Click the **OrderDate** field.	The Property Sheet should still be open.
c) In the Property Sheet pane, click **Format**.	A list of available formats appears.
d) Click **Long Date**.	
e) Run the query.	The Query now shows the full month name. In fact, you might need to widen the column to see the whole thing.
4. Format the Order Date field using a custom date format.	On second thought, you'd rather use a format like 11.23.2016 for the field, but it's not in the default options. You can use a custom format instead.
a) In Query Design View, click the **OrderDate** field.	
b) In the Property Sheet pane, select **Long Date**.	You'll replace the existing Format field.
c) Type **mm.dd.yyyy**, then press **Enter**.	Access inserts a backslash before each dot in the format. This is called an escape *character*, and informs the query to display the next character literally rather than recognizing it as a special formatting character.
d) Run the query.	The dates are now formatted as digits, with leading zeros and dots to separate month, day, and year.

Do This	How & Why
5. Save the query.	
6. Close all open objects and the database.	

Assessment: Modifying queries

1. What field type can't you choose a pre-made format option for in the Property Sheet pane? Choose the best response.

    - Date/Time
    - Number
    - Text
    - All of the above

2. To sort by multiple values, you might need to rearrange the order of the fields in your query. True or false?

    - True
    - False

3. It's often better to hide a query field rather than just deleting it. True or false?

    - True
    - False

4. One of the entries in your CustomerName list is "Century Grocers." Which VBA string function would display it as "Century" in a query?

    - Left([CustomerName],7)
    - Right([CustomerName],7)
    - Trim([CustomerName])
    - Ucase([CustomerName])

Module C: Using calculated fields

Many queries simply display data pulled from a table, while others use *calculated fields* generated within the query itself. A calculated field usually is still ultimately based in data from a table, but the query transforms the source data into another form according to the calculation.

You will learn:

- Why calculated fields should be used in queries instead of tables
- When you might want to use a calculated field
- How to create calculated fields in Expression Builder

Why to use calculated fields in queries

Like many elements in Access, or database design in general, you don't just need to know how to create calculated fields. You also need to know why they're created, and when it is or isn't appropriate. To understand why it's so common to create calculated fields in queries, consider the role of a table. As you probably know, tables are primarily there to store raw data that will be used as a source for the queries, reports, and forms you create later.

Technically you can create calculated fields in a table. Sometimes for legal or auditing purposes you might need to create and store a calculated value because it has to be created from a set of data *as it exists at a certain point in time*. Think about tracking the price of an item over the life of that item. Different customers pay different amounts depending when they made the purchase. If you change the item price, it's important that it doesn't change older sales records. To do that your database needs something that ties an item's price to a point in time. A common solution to this issue is to create a table (Named "Archived Prices," maybe) that contains information about a price, the product, and a starting and ending date.

In that example, though, you're storing the result of a calculation rather than a field that has the formula itself. The difference is significant. A general rule of thumb is that if you have all the pieces of the calculation already stored, don't create a table field that also stores it. It becomes too easy for data to get out-of-sync.

Not all calculations are equally important, and just philosophically speaking, it's a best practice to keep our table structures as clean and simple as possible. When you need a calculated field, you should default to creating it in a query rather than the underlying table, and then use the query as the basis for a form, report, or another query.

Calculated field types

A calculated field is any query field that doesn't simply return a value stored in the underlying data source. Actually, a query can also be the source for another query, but to keep it simple just consider tables as data sources for now.

While the term "calculation" might immediately have you thinking of numeric functions, in truth a calculation is any manipulation of the data source data. Some common examples to calculated fields in a query include:

- Displaying a 4-digit year or the name of the month for a Date/Time field
- Creating custom flags for Yes/No data
- Substituting a different value to display for null fields
- Joining two or more Text fields into one string
- Displaying a status value based on a certain threshold in another field

Creating calculated fields

Any query in Access can contain any number of calculated fields. Typically, the calculated field will contain output based on some function we apply to data in the underlying data source. To start creating a calculated field, click in a blank Field cell in the query window.

- If you know the expression you want to use, you can start typing the function name. Where appropriate, add the field names you need inside square brackets.

  The [ ] tells Access to return for each record in the query recordset, and to base that calculated value on the underlying field value in each individual record.

- If you don't know exactly how to construct the arguments for the function you need to use, right-click in the cell and choose **Build**.

  This will open Expression Builder, which will give you the ability to find functions and display placeholders for the values you'll need to pass.

- If you don't even know which function to use, or if a function even exists to do what you want to do, try using your favorite web search engine to narrow down the possibilities.

  Starting with "How do I _____?" usually produces some good results. If you search for *"How do I add days to a date in Access?"*, one of the first results you'll likely get will be an explanation on the Microsoft MSDN site.

Using Expression Builder

Expression Builder allows you to access all of the functions built into Access, and use them to assemble an expression. Even if you already know what expressions you want to use, you might still want to use Expression Builder anyway just to avoid mistyping anything.

The Expression Builder window

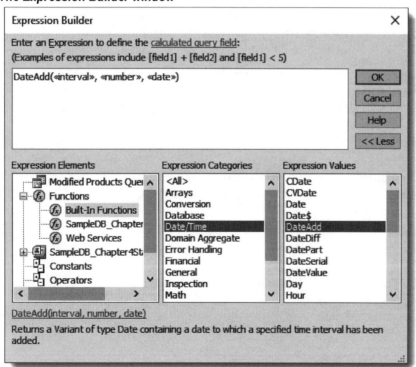

Every expression is different, so it's probably easiest to think of an example while looking at the abstract process. For example, imagine that employees are eligible for health insurance 90 days after their Hire Date. You want to create a calculated field to show the value in the query.

1. Right-click a field cell and choose **Build**.
2. From the Expression Elements list, click a listed element.
   In this case, you'll expand Functions and click **Built-in Functions**.
   The Expression Categories list will show categories related to that element.
3. In the Expression Categories list, click a category.
   To add days to a date, click **Time/Date**.
4. In the Expression Values list, double-click the value you want.
   In this case, you'll double-click **DateAdd**.
   Access will add the function name and <<placeholder>> arguments to the top pane of the window.
5. Replace each placeholder value with your own values.

   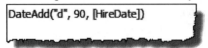

In this case "d" represents "days." If you were adding years, you'd use "yyyy" instead.

6. Click **OK**.
7. In the Field name, replace the default "Expr#" field name with one of your choosing.

   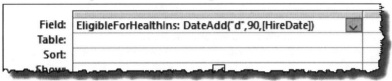

Creating calculated Yes/No fields

One popular use of calculated fields is to format Yes/No values. While that field type can represent any sort of binary value, the only built-in formatting options Access gives you are Yes/No, True/False, and On/Off. If you want to use anything else, you can't set it in the Property Sheet pane, but you can do it with a calculated field.

A Yes/No expression that returns "Can Drive" or a blank space

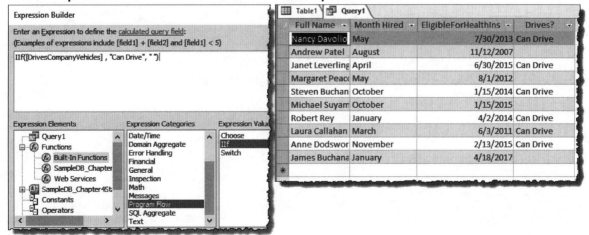

1. Click in the field you want to create.
2. Open Expression Builder.
3. Choose **Functions > Built-In Functions > Program Flow**.
4. Double-click **IIf**.

5. Replace the placeholders.

   a) Replace <<**expression**>> with the Yes/No field name.
      Don't forget to use square brackets.

   b) Replace <<**truepart**>> with whatever you want to represent a "Yes" value.

   c) Replace <<**falsepart**>> with whatever you want to represent a "No" value.

6. Click **OK**.

7. In the Field name, replace the default "Expr#" field name with one of your choosing.

Calculated text fields

As it simplest, a calculated text field could be joining two or more strings to display one value. If a report is going to show a customer's full name, we could create a calculated field with an expression like

```
[FirstName] & " " & [LastName]
```

The & character is how we join strings in calculated fields. Most often, Access will even convert values for you that aren't stored as strings automatically.

```
[LastName] & " had a review score of " & [LastReviewScore]
```

...would work as a calculated field even if `[LastReviewScore]` is stored as a number. If you need to manage the way the conversion works, say with date/time fields for example, explore the Format function on MSDN, which provides several conversion formats and allows for user-created custom formats, too.

Exercise: Using calculated fields

Do This	How & Why
1. Create a new query.	To make the exercise easier, you'll design a query that only returns a limited number of order records. This way, it will be easier for you to focus on how calculations affect individual records.
a) On the Create tab, click **Query Design**.	
b) Add the **Orders, Order Details,** and **Products** tables to the data source list.	Close the Show Table window when you're done.
c) From the Orders table, add **OrderDate** and **CustomerID** to the query.	Double-click them.
d) From the Order Details table, add **UnitPrice** and **Quantity**.	
e) From the Products table, add **Reorder Level**.	

Do This	How & Why
f) In the **Criteria** cell for the CustomerID field, enter `Like B*`.	This criteria will return only records for customers starting with the letter B. It's an arbitrary restriction to reduce the total number of records.
g) Test the query.	It returns 199 results. All are from customers starting with the letter B.
2. Replace the OrderDate field with a calculated field.	All you really want to show is the month of the order date, so you'll use a calculated field.
a) Right-click the **OrderDate** field cell in the query, and choose **Build**.	The Expression Builder window opens.
b) In the Expression Elements pane, expand the **Functions** node and click **Built-In Functions**.	Lists appear in both the Expression Categories and Expression Values fields.
c) In the Expression Categories list, click **Date/Time**.	
d) In the Expression Values list, double-click **Month**,	Access inserts the Month expression in the top field, with a `<<date>>` placeholder.
e) Click **<<date>>** and type `[OrderDate]`.	To replace the placeholder with the OrderDate field.
f) Click **OK**.	To close Expression Builder. The calculated field is inserted in the query.
g) Run the query.	It shows the month, but only as a number. You want the month name.
3. Edit the calculated field to show the month name.	The MonthName function will return the name of a numerical month. You can wrap that around the existing function.
a) Enter Design View.	
b) Open Expression Builder for the Month field.	Right-click it and choose **Build**.
c) Edit the expression to read `MonthName(Month([OrderDate]))`.	You can type it in directly, or delete the existing expression and start over.

Chapter 4: Queries / Module C: Using calculated fields

Do This	How & Why
d) Click **OK**.	
e) Run the query.	*(query result showing Expr1 column with month names August, August, September, September, September and Customer column with Blondel père et fils, Blondel père et fils, Berglunds snabbköp, Berglunds snabbköp, Berglunds snabbköp)* Now it shows month names.
4. Create a field that tells you when a product needs to be reordered.	You can use a calculated field that tells you if a product's current stock is below the reorder level.
a) Right-click in the first blank field and choose **Build**.	To open Expression Builder.
b) Insert the **IIf** function.	Click **Functions > Built-In Functions > Program Flow**, then double-click **IIf**.
c) Replace the <<**expression**>> placeholder with `[ReorderLevel] > [UnitsInStock]`.	
d) Replace the <<**truepart**>> placeholder with `"Reorder Now!"`.	
e) Replace the <<**falsepart**>> placeholder with `"Inventory OK"`.	`IIf([ReorderLevel] > [UnitsInStock], "Reorder Now!", "Inventory OK")` `IIf(expression, truepart, falsepart)`
f) Click **OK**.	To close Expression Builder.
g) Run the query.	*(query result showing er Leve and Expr2 columns: 0 Inventory OK, 30 Reorder Now!, 15 Inventory OK, 0 Inventory OK)*
5. Create a calculated field using a math function.	You'll display the Unit Price field rounded to the nearest dollar.
a) In Design View, right-click the **Unit Price** field and click **Build**.	To enter Expression Builder.
b) Delete the existing expression.	You'll start from scratch.
c) Add the **Round** expression.	It's in **Functions > Built-In Functions > Math >** .

Do This	How & Why
d) Replace the placeholders as shown.	Round([UnitPrice], 0) Round(number, [precision]) The UnitPrice field is the number, and 0 precision means it will have zero decimal places.
e) Click **OK**.	To close Expression Builder.
f) Run the query.	Access displays an error message. Since there is more than one table in the query with a UnitPrice field, you need to be more specific which one you mean.
g) Click **OK**.	To close the error message.
h) Edit the expression to read `Round([Order Details].[UnitPrice],0)`.	Place the table name (in square brackets) in front of the field name, and separate them with a decimal point. You can use Expression Builder, or do it right in the Field cell.
i) Run the query.	Now it works properly. One problem is that all your new fields show "Expr#" header. Another is that the rounded price field isn't formatted as currency: it's just a number.
6. Rename all the calculated fields to something more useful to users.	For example, `Month`, `Unit Price`, and `Reorder?`
7. Save the query as `Calculated Query`.	
8. Close all open objects and the database.	

Calculated Query

Month	Customer	Unit Price	Quanti	Reorder Leve	Reorder?
August	Blondel père et fils	31	30	0	Inventory OK
August	Blondel père et fils	12	20	30	Reorder Now!
September	Berglunds snabbköp	16	16	15	Inventory OK
September	Berglunds snabbköp	44	15	0	Inventory OK
September	Berglunds snabbköp	35	8	5	Inventory OK
September	Berglunds snabbköp	12	25	5	Inventory OK
September	Berglunds snabbköp	4	12	0	Inventory OK
September	Berglunds snabbköp	19	20	20	Inventory OK
September	Berglunds snabbköp	6	30	25	Inventory OK
September	B's Beverages	8	30	25	Reorder Now!
September	B's Beverages	27	9	30	Reorder Now!
October	Blondel père et fils	14	60	5	Inventory OK

Assessment: Using calculated fields

1. Why is it better to put calculated fields in queries than in tables? Choose all that apply.

   - It's easy for data to become out of sync due to later changes.
   - It's much more work to enter a calculated field in a table than in a query.
   - Table data should never be edited directly.
   - Table structures should be kept as simple as possible.

2. In Expression Builder, how would you write a reference to the EmployeeID field?

   - "EmployeeID"
   - (EmployeeID)
   - <<EmployeeID>>
   - [EmployeeID]

3. In a calculated text field, you don't need to do anything special to add a numeric value to a text string. True or false?

   - True
   - False

Summary: Queries

You should now know:

- How to create an assortment of basic queries, including both select queries and action queries
- How to change the presentation, formatting, and sort order of queries
- How to use Expression Builder to design calculated fields in a query

Synthesis: Queries

You want some data about who you're selling individual products to.

1. Open `SampleDB_SynthesisStart`.
2. Design a query that will reports how many orders you've received for each product in the Beverages category.
   - You'll need to add the tables to give you a suitable relationship.
   - Be sure to use the CategoryName field, not the Category field.
   - Sort the results by customer, and then by product name.
   - Hide the CategoryName field.
3. Change the query to display the number times each customer has ordered a specific product.
   Use a totals function, adding a field if necessary.
4. Name the totals row `# of orders`.
   Use the Caption property.
5. Add a calculated Yes/No field that specifies whether the company is in Germany.
   - Use the `IIf` function.
   - Remember to use quotes where appropriate in the expression.
6. Change the query to return results from a user-specified category.
   Set a parameter.
7. Use the query to make a new table.
   You'll have to change its query type.
8. Close the database.

Chapter 5: Forms

You will learn:

- How to create simple forms
- About form design
- How to use form controls

Module A: Creating simple forms

Two basic form types are bound and unbound forms. Bound forms are tied to a particular data source like a table or query. Unbound forms are used to accomplish other types of application-specific tasks.

You will learn how to:

- Create simple forms
- Use different form views for different functions
- Create bound and unbound forms both from scratch and using the Form Wizard

About forms

Tables are the foundations of data storage. Queries are objects that extract data from those tables in any way we desire. So where do forms fit in?

There are four basic operations that a database handles; it can *create*, *retrieve*, *update*, and *delete* (CRUD) data. Queries take care of data retrieval, and forms handle creation, updating, and deletion. But that's only part of the story. We can design other types of forms for any purpose we want. A form doesn't have to just do its CRUD work to be useful in Access.

There are two basic form types:

- *Bound* forms are tied to a particular data source, such as a table or query.
- *Unbound* forms are used to accomplish other application-specific tasks.

Basic form design options

Access offers some basic form types directly from the ribbon—in other words, from scratch—to pre-built forms, with all their controls already created. Consider any of these as a starting point, realizing that almost everything about your form can be customized as needed.

If you're starting from scratch with no other objects open in Access, in the Create tab's Forms section, you'll have the **Form Design** and **Blank Form** buttons available in the ribbon. You can use either method to create a blank form. The initial view is different, and using the Form Design button gives an extra view (Datasheet); other than that, they have the same effect.

> **Note:** You can see the Datasheet view of any form by right-clicking the form, then choosing **Datasheet View**, even if the choice isn't available in the View button's drop-down list.

Think of these two buttons as your "canvas" for you to exercise your creative magic by applying form properties and controls.

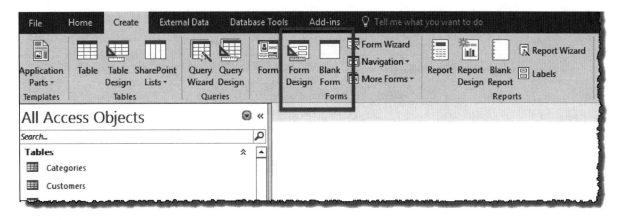

Form views

Let's take a minute to go through the different views available for a form. Which view you use will determine what you can do with your controls and the design of the form, and what sort of data you'll see. You can see each view of the form by going to the Design tab's Form Layout Tools section and choosing the View drop-down list.

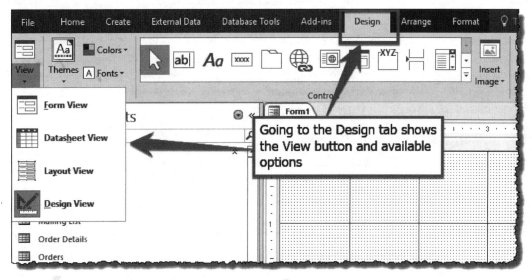

You can display forms in any of four views:

- *Form View* gives you access to the full detail of your form. You can see all the sections and change their properties, so if you've created a Header or Footer section, this view is the easiest place to edit that, and there are some form properties that can only be changed from here and not in Layout view.

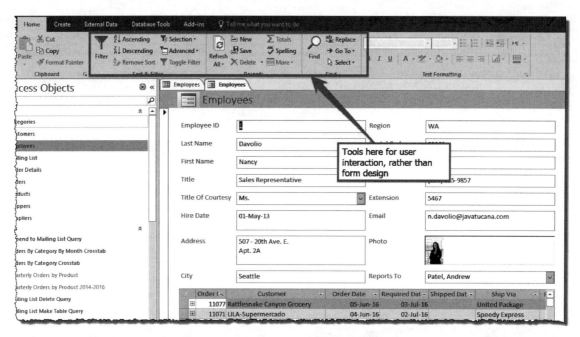

- *Datasheet View* lets you see the exact same look as the Datasheet view in a table or a query. If you don't see a Datasheet View option in the View button drop-down, check the Form's **Allow Datasheet View** property, and set it to **Yes**. You should then see the Datasheet View option. Datasheet View is used quite a bit for subforms (forms contained in other forms) as a concise way to present related data. If a main form shows one customer record, you could add a subform in Datasheet View that displays all the customer's orders at one time.

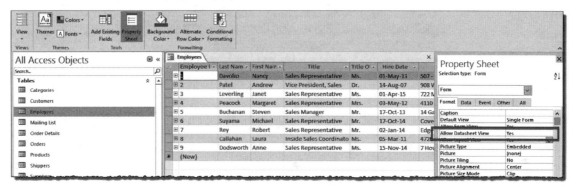

- *Layout View* offers the widest range of flexibility of all views, in that you can edit your form and see actual live data simultaneously. For some developers who create applications with more "bells and whistles," this view might seem counterintuitive. For example, it's often assumed that we should write our code, compile it, and then run it, right? Wrong! Layout View makes this much easier.

In Layout View, your form is actually running, and you can still change the form design at the same time. Would you like to move controls around? Align them? Move forward or backward to see actual data? Yes, yes, and yes. If there are things you can't do in Layout View, Access will pop up a helpful message telling you to make the switch.

- *Design View* gives you access to all of your form's details. You can see all the sections and change their properties, so if you've created a Header or Footer section, this view is the easiest place to edit that, and there are some form properties that can *only* be changed from here and *not* in Layout view.

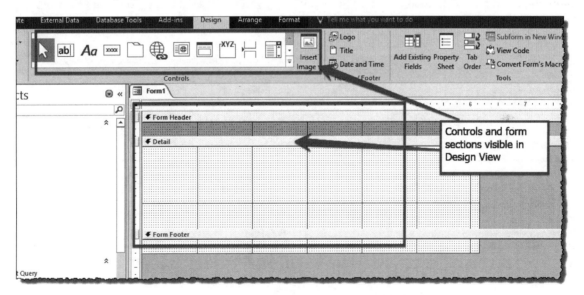

Bound and unbound form controls

Any time you need to interact directly with the user, a form is probably the best way to do it. A *bound* form is simply one where the *Record Source* property of the form is set. Usually, this value is the name of a table or a query. It's also possible to set a record source using a custom-created SQL query, if there's no existing table or query that works for you.

The impact of setting the record source is that the form is now bound to that set of data. Now you begin to add controls to the form, and set those controls to be bound to specific fields in the data source. Controls become bound controls by having their *Control Source* property set. The value you'll see in a control source property is a field name in the record source data. You have the freedom to choose, and not every field in the data source has to be represented by a control. Once your controls are cited on the form, users can easily add, edit, or delete records from the data source if allowed to do so. This part can be configured in the form's properties as well.

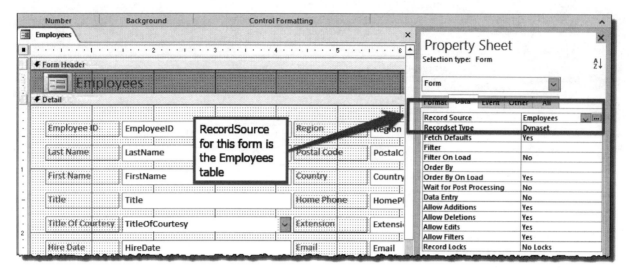

The other side of this equation is that we have unbound forms and unbound controls. This means that the Record Source property (for a form) or the Control Source property (for a control) isn't set. Using unbound forms for data manipulation provides greater flexibility, at the expense of having to do more of the design work manually, most often using more sophisticated coding techniques. Unbound forms are favored by many programmers when the data is from a source other than Access (for example, a network-based SQL server). This is helpful for increased processing speed and for multi-user locking issues.

Unbound forms can also be used to present data in a pleasing visual format. A splash screen that displays at application startup is a common use of an unbound form. It introduces the user to the application, gives them something to look at while background components load, and can display legal disclaimers and so on. There's no table or query data involved.

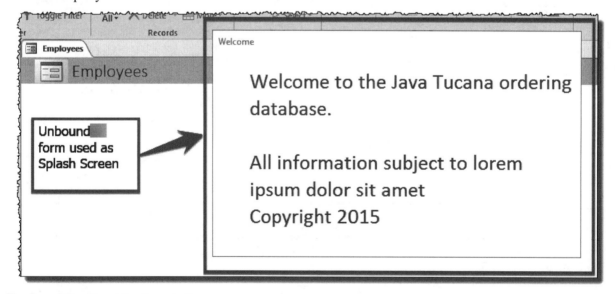

The Form Wizard and the Form button

You may also encounter form types in which the record source is already set. For example, if you use the Form Wizard, part of its process is to walk you through choosing a table or query as your record source, and then creating controls to go with it. If you use the Blank Form or Form Design buttons to create the form, you set the record source yourself.

The easiest way to create your own controls is to use the Form button. Access controls control creation according to context—the object you're working on at the time. Thus, you can also use the Form button when you have a table or query open. On the Create tab, in the Forms group, click the **Form** button. Access creates a form that's already bound to the query or table you were working in. It opens in Layout view, but you're still free to customize from this starting point, as you would with any other form.

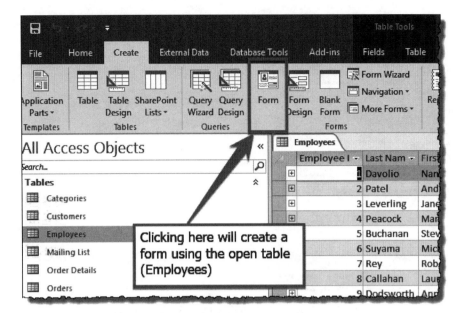

The Form Wizard button should be available whenever you need it. The wizard walks you through the creation of a bound form, including your choice of fields and the initial style of the form. There are four choices available, all functionally equivalent but visually different.

You can also use the wizard to create forms that walk users through related data. All it takes to get started is to choose more than one table or query and decide which fields you want. Technically you can do this with any two data sources, but it only makes practical sense to use data that's related.

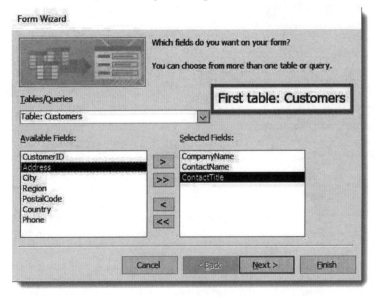

The wizard displays a screen prompting you to choose how to present the data. Most often, you would probably want to view it by one side of the relationship.

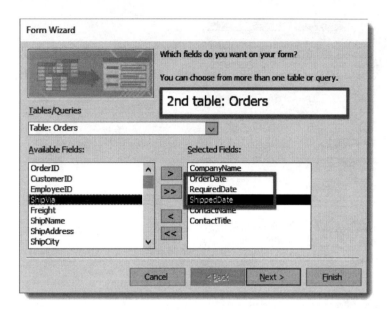

You pick from a subform, which is another form that's embedded in the main form, or a linked form, where a button is created on the main form that opens the child form separately.

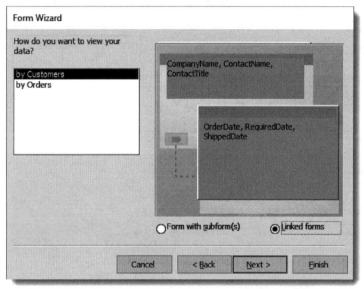

In both cases, the wizard sets it up so that the information is passed between forms. So, if you're viewing Customers (in this case, one side of the relationship), the subform or linked form with Order information will show only the records related to the customer on the parent form.

You might wish to dig into the design of the child form. Access typically doesn't make the layout pretty. Adjusting the size of the textboxes is probably going to be one of the first things you do. The wizard makes guesses as to appearance, but it's best to look at the average length of the text for each field and decide for yourself.

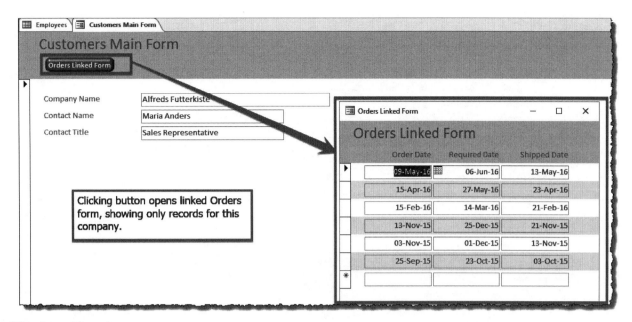

Other bound form types

In the Create tab's Forms group are three other options for creating forms. There's no wizard involved; however, the process is still quick and easy. All three methods automatically create a form using the table or query selected in the Navigation pane, and all are editable after creation.

- *Datasheet*: This is the exact same look and feel as a table or query datasheet, but with the added benefit of being able to eliminate fields you don't want displayed.

- *Multiple Items*: If you want to see more than one record at a time, this form displays multiple records in rows. It's similar to a Datasheet form in that respect, but much better looking than the relatively plain Datasheet view.

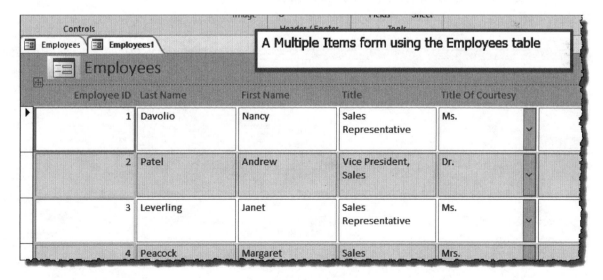

- *Split*: If you want the benefits of having both a multiple-records view and a large editing area, the Split form gives you both views in one place: a datasheet on the bottom to select a record, and editable controls on top.

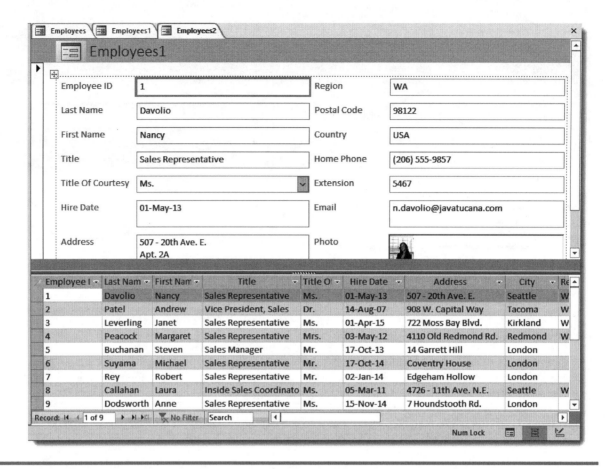

Exercise: Creating a form with the Form Wizard

In this exercise, you'll use the Form Wizard to create a form using two tables as data sources.

Do This	How & Why
1. Open `SampleDB_Chapter5Start.accdb` from the data folder.	
2. On the Create tab, click **Form Wizard**.	In the Forms group. 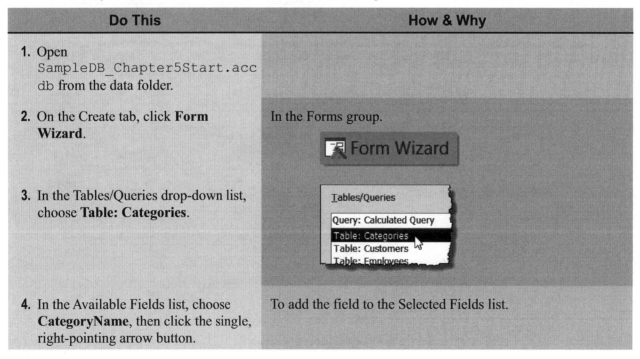
3. In the Tables/Queries drop-down list, choose **Table: Categories**.	
4. In the Available Fields list, choose **CategoryName**, then click the single, right-pointing arrow button.	To add the field to the Selected Fields list.

Do This	How & Why
5. Add the **Description** field to the Selected Fields list.	Use the same method as in step 3. 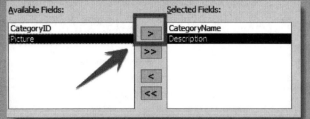
6. From the Tables/Queries drop-down list, choose **Table: Products**.	
7. From the Available Fields list, select the **ProductName**, **QuantityPerUnit**, **UnitPrice**, **UnitsInStock**, and **UnitsOnOrder** fields, adding each to the Selected Fields list.	Click the right-pointing arrow to add each one to the list.
8. Advance to the next wizard pane.	Click **Next**.
9. If necessary, choose **by Categories**, and click **Form with subform(s)**.	To specify how to display the data. The Wizard will create a form to navigate through Categories records and related Products.
10. Advance two wizard panes.	Click **Next** twice.
11. Title the form `Categories Main Form`, and leave the "Products Subform" title as it is.	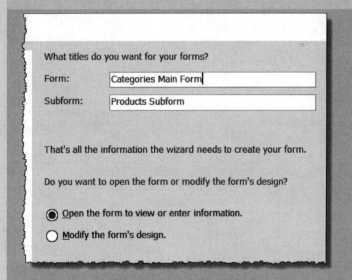
12. Click **Finish**. Close the form after you look at it.	The new form is displayed. You can click the navigation buttons at the bottom of the main form to scroll through Category records. The Products information on the subform is automatically synced to the displayed Category record.
13. Double-click the **Suppliers** table.	You'll need to expand the Tables node in the Navigation pane. The Suppliers table opens in Datasheet view. You'll create a form using the Form button, then add a filter.

Do This	How & Why
14. On the Create tab, click **Form**. In the Forms group. Access creates and opens a form using Supplier data. 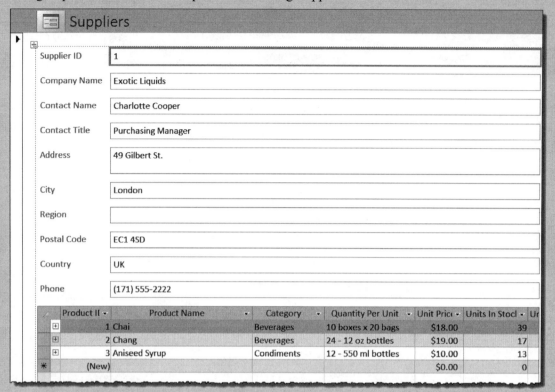	
15. From the Property Sheet on the right, click the drop-down list at the top of the box, and click **Form**.	This switches the Property Sheet to display Form properties. 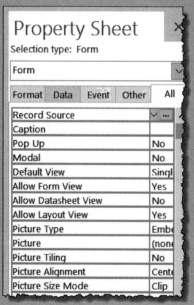

Do This	How & Why
16. Click the Data tab, and add a Filter so that this form only displays Supplier records from Germany, Italy, France, and the UK.	In the Filter property box, enter the following expression: `[Country] in ("Germany","Italy","France","UK")` This selects only records for which the Country value matches one of the four choices entered here.
17. Change the Filter On Load property to **Yes**.	Directly below the filter.
18. Close and reopen the form to activate the filter.	To activate the filter. Closing the form causes Access to prompt you to save it.
19. Name the form `Selected European Suppliers`, then click **OK**.	 The form now shows only those records (approximately 10) that are let through the filter. You'll explore the functionality available in different form views.
20. Click **View**.	Note that there is no Datasheet view available for this form.
21. In the Property Sheet, on the Format tab, change value of the Allow Datasheet View property to **Yes**.	You will need to switch to design view to access the form properties.
22. Click **View**.	A Datasheet View option now appears.
23. Click **Datasheet View**.	To display the output.
24. Switch to **Layout View**, then scroll through the form records, and notice what's available in the ribbon.	From the View button. You can see live data, but you can still change elements of the form.
25. Click on the **Country** text box, then click on **Font Color**, and change the color to whatever one suits you.	In the menu. The running form displays the new color.
26. Right-click anywhere on the form (but outside a data input box), and choose **Form View**.	You can still see the live data, but the ribbon has changed. The font color choice you made in Layout view is still in effect, but your ribbon now displays a different toolset.
27. Navigate to the supplier ID 12 record.	The Company whose name starts with "Plutzer").

Do This	How & Why
28. In the subform, click on the **Unit Price** column header; in the Records group, click on **More**, and choose **Hide Fields**.	*(menu shown: More ▼ — Add From Outlook, Save As Outlook Contact, Row Height..., Subdatasheet, Hide Fields, Unhide Fields, Freeze Fields, Unfreeze All Fields, Field Width)* The Unit Price field is now hidden. You'll re-display it.
29. Click on **More**, then choose **Unhide Fields**, check **Unit Price**, and click **Close**.	The Unit Price field reappears in the subform.
30. Save and close the form.	

Assessment: Forms

1. True or false? Of the four basic database operations, forms can handle creation, deletion, and bilateral recalcitrance.

   - True
   - False

2. Which of the following statements about forms is correct?

   - An unbound form is always tied to multiple tables.
   - A bound form is tied to a specific data source.
   - A query is a type of form bound to a specific data source.
   - A split form is used to input data into multiple tables.

3. Layout view allows you to edit your form and see actual live data simultaneously.

   - True
   - False

4. Which view allows you to edit all form properties as well as a header/footer?

   - Datasheet view
   - Layout view
   - Form view
   - Design view

5. When adding fields to a form, you select one or more field names in the Selected Fields list and add them to the Available Fields list.

   - True
   - False

Module B: Form design

After you've created a form, you still have complete control over its look, feel, and functionality, as well as that of its controls.

You will learn how to:

- Understand form properties
- Work with form sections

Displaying form properties

The Property Sheet displays as a pane in the Access window. It is the nerve center of any form or control's display and behavior characteristics.

1. In Design or Layout view, click **Property Sheet**.
    In the Design tab's Tools group.

2. Observe the Property Sheet pane.
    Access automatically display the sheet corresponding to the control you've selected while in Design view or Layout view. At any time, you can choose what properties you want to see in the drop-down list at the top. Regardless of the form's name, the form itself will always be listed simply as "Form."

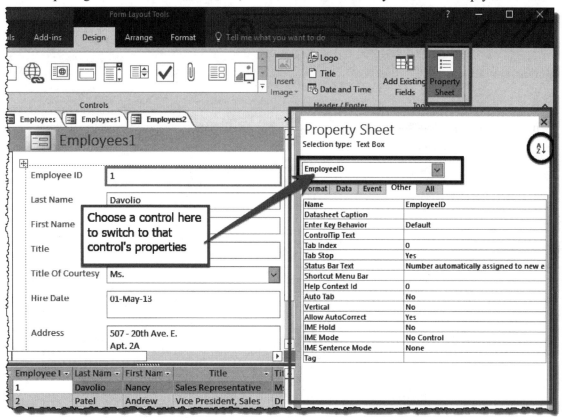

3. To display properties in alphabetical order, click the Sort button.
    Just below the pane's Close button. This Sort button toggles between its default arrangement and alphabetical order.

Commonly used form properties

In the context of form properties, it can be overwhelming to see all the tabs and editable values on any property sheet and know where to start. Thus, it's simplest to break them down by tabs and their groups of functions.

 Note: Some of these properties can be changed *only* in Design view, so you might be required to switch to that view from the Property Sheet in Layout view.

The Format tab controls the appearance of the form. There are plenty of form sizing options here. Some of the more interesting ones include:

- *AutoResize*: When set to **True**, the form automatically opens sizes to display a full record in Form view. Otherwise, the form opens to the last saved size.
- *BorderStyle*: You can choose from **None**, **Thin**, **Sizable**, or **Dialog**. Sizable is the default, but if you're designing a form that only works at a certain size, None prevents users from resizing it.
- *ScrollBars*: Although it's not technically a resizing option, the **Scroll Bars** option allows for content that doesn't fit in the current window size. You can choose to have horizontal or vertical scroll bars, both, or none at all.

In bound forms, you might also want to control what displays for users to navigate through records:

- *NavigationButtons*, *DividingLines*, and *RecordSelectors*: Set the value to **Yes** to display them. DividingLines refers to the lines between records. RecordSelectors is the visual indication that a record is selected; setting it to **No** still allows users to select a record, but the only visual cue of having done so is that the cursor appears in the selected control.
- *NavigationCaption*: A string is displayed to the left of the Navigation buttons.
- *AllowFormView*, *AllowDatasheetView*, and *AllowLayoutView*: Each property can be set to **Yes** to allow user access. Think about this setting as configuring what's available during database design. If you plan to lock down the design when you're finished and ready to release this as an application, you can lock down the interface (in other words, disable menus, Design view, and so on), set a startup form, and save an .ACCDE file.

The Data tab is where you choose what and how records are displayed. Some common properties include:

- *RecordSource*: The table, query, or custom SQL statement that provides form records. To create an SQL statement, click the ellipsis (…) button on the RecordSource property. Doing so displays the Access Query Builder.
- *Filter*: Shows a subset of records designated by the RecordSource property. For example, if your RecordSource is the Customers table, you could make the form show only customers from Italy by setting the Filter property to `[Country]="Italy"`.
- *OrderBy*: Displays records in a specified order. Using the example above, you could display Italian customers in order, according to city, by specifying `[City]` in the OrderBy property. A sort in ascending order is the default. To reverse this, add `DESC` after the field name.
- *AllowAdditions*, *AllowDeletions*, *AllowEdits*: Setting these properties to **Yes** restricts users' ability to add, delete, or update records, respectively.

Form sections

In Design view, you can display and customize the Form Header, Detail, and Form Footer sections of a form. You can also add other custom sections.

The *Form Header* and *Form Footer* sections display the same information regardless of what record the form is displaying. Typical uses include a company logo or the date and time in the Form Header, or some legal/disclaimer information about proper data use at the Form Footer.

Note: The default Form Footer doesn't show anything in it, in fact, it looks like there's nothing there at all! To use it, drag down from the bottom of the Form Footer section header to display the same grid visible in the Details section.

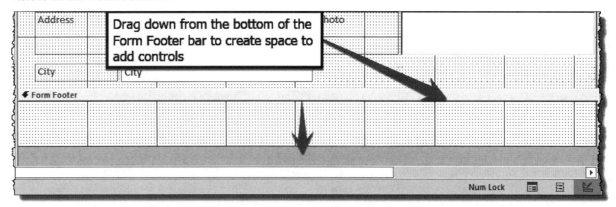

Although it's possible to put bound controls in the Form Header, or the Form Footer, it's not standard practice to do so. The main thing to know about the form header and footer is that they stay on the screen all the time while the Details section scrolls up and down.

Additionally, the header and footer sections have a few properties that the detail section does not.

- *Visible* is a Yes/No setting that determines whether to show either the header or the footer section.
- *Height* determines how tall the header or footer section is.
- *Back Color* allows you to set a different background color for the header and footer to differentiate it from the Details section.

The *Details* section is where the magic of your form happens. However, you only ever see one set of controls in this section, which represents the display of one record. When you choose different types of forms, that single set of controls you see in the Details section can repeat over and over. For example, here's the Design view of a multiple items form, and then the Form view that results.

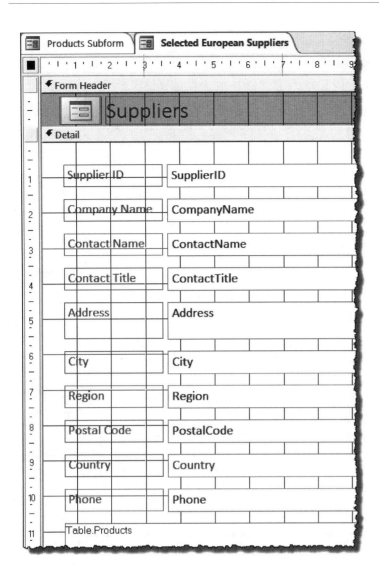

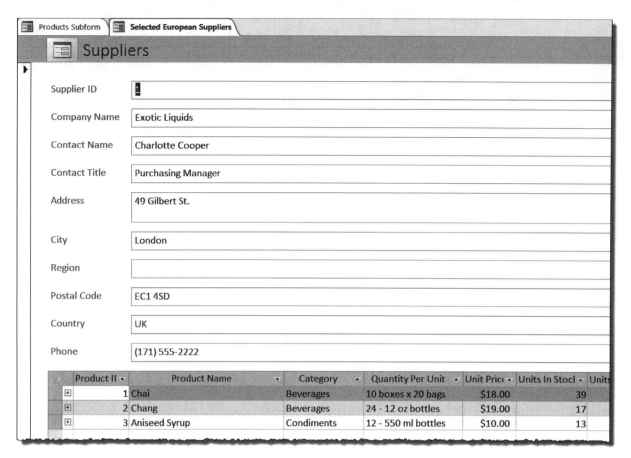

You can still manage what controls show up and how they look. Think of this as the template for a single record. There is no need to add a second control that's bound to the same field in the details section, unless you actually want to display the same data twice.

Exercise: Designing a form

You'll design a form, including its sections and the elements in each section.

Do This	How & Why
1. Open the **Selected European Suppliers** form in Design view.	From the Navigation pane's Forms node, and click **Design View**.
2. Change the form's properties as follows:	
a) If necessary, open the form's property sheet.	If it isn't already displayed, click **Property Sheet**.
b) Display the form properties, if necessary.	Click the drop-down list at the top of the property sheet, and click **Form**.
c) On the Data tab of the property sheet, locate the Allow Edits property.	If you want to restrict changes to the data, you can do so here.
d) Change the Allow Edits property to **No**.	

Do This	How & Why
e) Switch to Form view.	Click **View** > **Form View**.
f) Attempt to change the value for Company Name in any record.	The value cannot be changed.
g) Switch to Layout view.	The Filtered button to the right of the form navigation is activated. The form currently displays filtered records. **▼ Filtered**
h) Change the Allow Filters property to **No**.	On the Data tab of the form's Property Sheet.
i) Switch the view to activate the property change.	Users no longer have the ability to turn the filter on and off.
j) Reset the Allow Filters property to **Yes**, change the form view again, and then verify that users can again turn the filter on and off.	Look for the Filtered icon.

3. Experiment with the form's Data Entry property:

    a) Set the Data Entry property to **Yes**, and observe the form.

    In Form view. Blank form fields are displayed, because Data Entry only allows for the inputting of new records but not displaying existing ones.

    b) Return to the Property Sheet, and change the Data Entry property back to **No**.

    c) Close the form without saving changes.

4. Create a new form with a custom RecordSource:

    a) On the Create tab, click **Form Design**.

    To create a new, blank form in Design view. The Design tab is also displayed.

    b) On the Data tab of the Form property sheet, click in the empty RecordSource box, then click [...] (More).

    The query builder opens with the Show Tables window open.

Do This	How & Why
c) On the Queries tab of the Show Table window, select **Customer Order Totals Query**, and click **Add**.	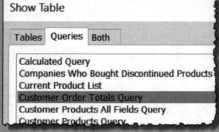
d) On the Tables tab, select the **Orders** table, then click **Add**.	
e) Close the Show Table window.	Click **Close**.

5. Add fields to the query:

   a) Double-click all three fields from the Customer Order Totals Query to add them to the field list.

   b) Add the OrderDate field from the Orders table to the field list.

   Double-click its name in the table.

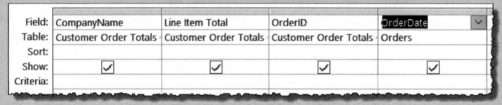

Do This	How & Why
c) Create a calculated field by entering the following expression in the first blank Field cell to the right of OrderDate: `DaysSinceOrder: DateDiff("d", [OrderDate],Date())`.	This will include a field with the number of days since the order was made, using the VBA Date( ) function that returns the current system date.
d) Click **Run**.	To see what records are included in the form.
e) Return to design view, and then click **Close**.	Click **Yes** to save when prompted. To close the query builder and save the generated SQL statement as the RecordSource of the form.

6. Set the OrderBy property for the new form:

   a) On the Data tab of the Form properties, sort the form with the earliest date first by entering `[OrderDate] DESC` in the Order By property.

   Because we don't have any bound controls on the form, we can't see the effect of the setting yet.

Do This	How & Why
b) Save the form as `Customer Order Totals`.	
7. Add a Form Footer section:	
a) If necessary, switch to Design view.	Click **View > Design View**.
b) Right-click on the Detail section header, and choose **Form Header/Footer** from the context menu.	To add these two new sections to the form.
8. Change properties of the header and footer sections:	
a) Drag the Detail section header bar down to create a taller Form Header section.	
b) Drag the bottom of the Form Footer bar down to create a taller Form Footer section.	
c) Change the back color of the Form Footer section by right-clicking anywhere in the section, and choosing **Fill/Back Color**. Choose a lighter color such as yellow or orange.	
d) Click the Form Header bar, and tehn, on the Design tab, click **Date and Time**, and then click **OK** to retain the default settings.	In the Header/Footer group.
e) Click View to display the new form.	It's still without bound controls, but the Form Header should display the date and time, and the colored Form Footer should be visible.
9. Save and close the form.	

Assessment: Form design

1. From which central location can you change form properties?
   - The Form Design pane
   - The Form Properties window
   - The Property Design window
   - The Property Sheet pane

2. By default, a form's properties are listed in alphabetical order.
   - True
   - False

3. Which of these statements is correct?
   - The Data tab is where you choose what and how records are displayed.
   - Setting a property's value to *No* means that users cannot select a record.
   - The Filter property shows a subset of records designated by the OrderBy property.
   - Double-clicking the Form Footer bar creates additional space to add controls.

4. Only one set of controls is displayed in the Details section, which in turn represents a single data record.
   - True
   - False

Module C: Form controls

Controls, or widgets, are the individual objects we drop in a form to display data. The foundation of this functionality is the bound control, which displays data from a field in a table or query.

You will learn how to:

- Use data binding controls
- Understand types of controls and their use
- Change the layout and tab order of form controls

About form controls

Controls are the individual objects we drop in a form to display data. The foundation of this functionality is the bound control, which displays data from a field in a table or query. You can leverage the layout tools that Access provides to make your forms look professional.

In general, think of a control as a form element that enables the display of gathered information in the most efficient way. For example, if you want a user to enter a string of letters and numbers, use a Text Box control. If you need Yes/No data, use a Checkbox control. If we need someone to choose from a list of options, we could use a Combo Box or List Box to present that list and enable selection. There are a wide variety of controls you can use in Access, and when putting together a form, it's best to start by considering the data type of the field you want to view or edit. This leads you toward the best and most efficient type of control to use and bind to that field.

The easiest way to create a form is with the Form Wizard or the Form button. For example, in the form shown in the figure, which is in Design view, notice that the Show Date Picker property is set to the value "For Dates."

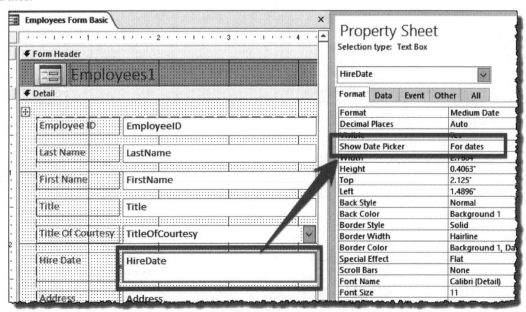

If this form is displaying a Date/Time field, the user has the opportunity to use a Date Picker by clicking the icon at the right side of the control. While this is technically just a Text Box control, setting the property we just discussed lets Access provide a visual cue to the user to help them enter appropriate data.

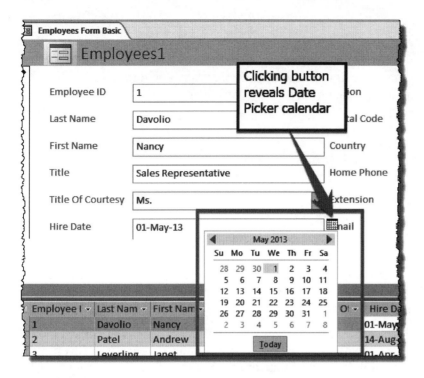

Adding bound controls to a form

Layout view and Design view offer a wide variety of controls in the Design tab's Controls group.

1. Hover over the controls in the Controls group.

    The name of the control is displayed, from which you can get some idea of the control's function.

2. Click the Control gallery's ⏷ (More button).

    All available controls are displayed. You'll also see the *Use Control Wizards* menu option. Leave this option enabled if you want Access to walk you through the process of data binding a control when you add it to the form.

3. Select a control to add to the form.
4. Draw the control of the form by clicking the destination location and dragging to the required size.

    You can always change the control's size after the fact by selecting, then resizing it. You can also copy existing controls to other locations on a form.

    > **Note:** Each control must have a unique name, so copying a control results in the new control being automatically and uniquely named by Access.

Adding controls from the field list

You can also add controls to a form and not have to worry about data binding by adding them from the field list.

1. Click **Add Existing Fields**; then, do one of the following:
   - Double-click a field to add its control (and label) to the form, at a location automatically chosen by Access, usually below or to the right of existing controls.
   - Click a field, then drag it onto the form, exactly where you would like it.
   In the Design tab's Tools group, to display the field list.

   The location where you drop the field will be where Access draws the upper left corner of the actual control, with a label to the left.

2. Experiment with dragging controls onto a form a few times to get a feel for where your label will end up relative to your bound control.

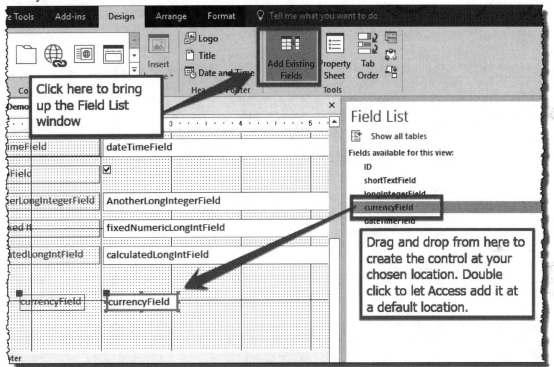

 Note: Any controls tied to Record Source data have their Control Source property set to the name of a field from the table or query, so if you're confused about why data are or aren't displayed in the control when you run the form, check the Control Source property first. Conversely, controls that aren't displaying data from the Record Source are called unbound. Labels are (usually) unbound, as are images like a company logo in a Form Header section. If it doesn't change when the record you're looking at changes, it's not a bound control.

Chapter 5: Forms / Module C: Form controls

Exercise: Adding form controls

In this exercise, you'll add controls to a form.

Do This	How & Why
1. Open the Customer Order Totals form.	In the Navigation pane's Forms node, right-click **Customer Order Totals**, and select **Design View**.
2. Add bound controls to the form:	
a) On the Design tab, click **Add Existing Fields**.	To displays the Field List window.
b) Drag the CompanyName field onto the form's Details section, near the middle of the second grid box from the left.	Access will draw a label to the left of the bound control, so you'll leave room here for that. If you need to move the control, drag it accordingly, and the label should follow.
c) Do the same with all the remaining query fields *except* OrderID.	
d) Change the form view to display live data.	Use Layout View or Form View. If the DaysSinceOrder field is showing date values in the early 1900s, there's a formatting problem! You'll fix that in the next step.
3. Change bound control formatting:	
a) Return to Design View, and click the bound Text Box control for DaysSinceOrder.	
b) On the Format tab of the property sheet, change the value to **General Number**.	Because you used a Date-related function, Access automatically formatted the calculated field as a Date. You're changing that in order to see a number.
a) Change the text of the label that goes with this control to **Days Since Order**, if necessary.	
4. View the data again to verify changes.	
a) Run the form in Layout View.	
b) Verify that the Days Since Order field now displays numerals.	
c) You might want to also drag the Company Name Text Box out to the right to see all the text in the field.	

Do This	How & Why
d) Make any other cosmetic property changes you want to the form.	
5. Save and close the form.	

Types of controls

The vast majority of user actions are typing into a text box, choosing from a set of options, and clicking (or tapping). Access provides a basic sets of controls that accommodate these gestures.

Text box and label controls

The Label control merely labels form controls. Access add labels automatically to almost every control you create on a form. If you want to change the label at any time, you're free to do so. The label is associated with the control, in that it moves with it if you reposition the control. Likewise, if you hide the control (through code or a macro), the associated label hides as well. If you somehow end up with a control that doesn't have a label (for example, if you accidentally delete it), you can add a new label, select the new label and the control, and Access gives you a choice on the Smart Tag menu that allows you to associate the two controls.

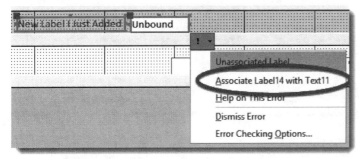

The workhorse among Access form controls is the standard Text Box control. By default, the text box allows any kind of character input. For example, if a control is bound to numeric data, any non-numeric input is disallowed when the user leaves the control or attempts to save the new or updated record, and Access displays an error message. If the control is bound to a Text or Date/Time field type, you can use the *Input Mask* property to restrict character entry and keep users from typing an invalid character string.

For example, let's say you had a field that displays an order number, and all the order numbers in your system are in the format "PL-19547-A"—in other words, a hyphen, five numbers, another hyphen, and one final letter. You could create an Input Mask for the form control that would restrict user input to only those character sets. But it's also a good idea to include some helpful text that lets the user know what's expected.

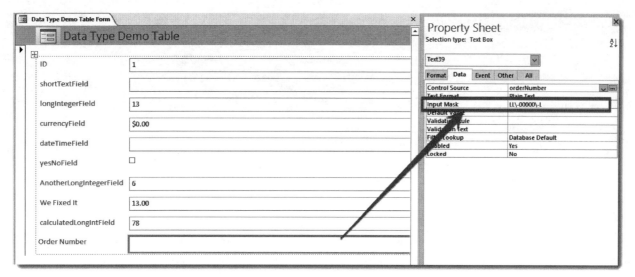

The Input Mask value "LL\-00000\-L" restricts input to the chosen format. "L" refers to a required letter; "0", a required number, and "\" to the left of a character means that the next character must be exactly what follows—any other input is rejected and not even displayed in the control. Thus, the user gets immediate feedback about what's valid. You can add a label for explanation, if you want to, or set the Control Tip Text to explain the desired format.

 Note: You can get more information on the Input Mask syntax (or any other property) on MSDN, or via the Help page.

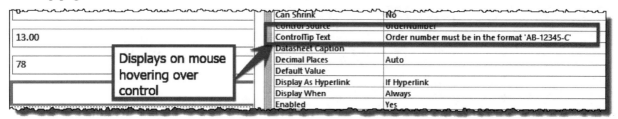

You might notice some properties of a bound control have the same names as the ones in the Field Properties section of the table. This is by design. If you set, for example, the Input Mask property in the field's Properties section from the table, it is automatically used for the form control if you add the control from the Field List box.

List controls

To present users with a list of choices for a field, use the Combo Box, List Box or Option Group. Which of these you employ is largely a matter of style and screen space:

- A *Combo Box* is a drop-down box with a pre-configured list of choices, so it takes up less space than the other list controls.

- A *List Box* displays its set of choices in a rectangular box whose size you can set, with scroll bars automatically becoming enabled when the number of choices exceeds available space.

- An *Option Group* creates a set of buttons in which the user is permitted to pick exactly one.

Using the List Box and Combo Box as bound controls requires setting their Row Source property. If you have the Use Control Wizards option enabled, Access walks you through this process when you draw a control on the form from the ribbon. You can have the values dynamically generated from another data source, type in a static list of values on your own, or use the third option to find a record based on the selected value. This last option is used when the selected item in the Combo Box is intended to trigger the display of related data on a subform or linked form.

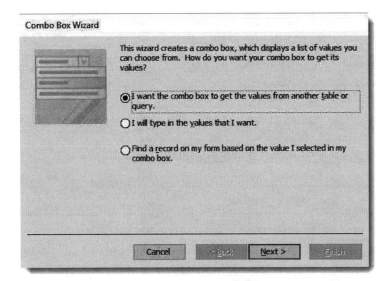

If the Row Source property binds you to a data source row, determine how many columns from that row you wish to display in the Combo Box, using the Column Count property. Access chooses that number of columns, starting with the first field in the table or query, from Row Source. Then set the Bound Column property that determines which column from the row is set as the value of the control. This is actually the process that the "Find a record..." option in the Combo Box Wizard leads you through.

One difference in the respective default settings of the List Box and Combo Box is what users are allowed to do. By default, users can still type their own entries into a Combo Box. However, you can set Limit To List to "No" to keep that from happening. With the List Box, there's no option for you to set, users can never add their own choices, and there's no way for you to change that.

The Option Group control actually shows up on the form as a Frame surrounding a set of Option Buttons—all as separate controls. During the Option Group Wizard process, you can instead choose to have check boxes or toggle buttons. If this is to be a bound control (in other words, to save the value of the chosen option in a field), set the Frame's Control Source property to the name of the field. The Frame is actually the only part of this "control" that's bound to the data—the Value property of the selected option control.

In this case, the Value can only be a number, which Access stores in the table it's bound to. If you want the Value to be text, you can create a separate table that maps numbers to text, and then bind the Frame to a table field of the "Lookup" type. Access then returns the appropriate text.

Consider this group of controls as pre-emptive data validation: It keeps the user from making a mistake by presenting only the choices you know to be valid.

Adding a command button

A powerful way to control a user action is by adding a command button to a form. When you use the command button's ability to run Macros or VBA code, almost any action is possible, and there's a wide variety of default actions included with Access.

The easiest way to discover available command options is to draw a button on your form with the **Use Control Wizards** menu option enabled. You're presented with a list of categories and available actions in each category, including navigating through records, opening and closing forms, running or emailing reports, running macros or queries, and many more. Depending on the action you choose, you're presented with other options to complete the configuration of the action. Access automatically executes the assigned action when the user clicks the button—all without your having to write any code whatsoever.

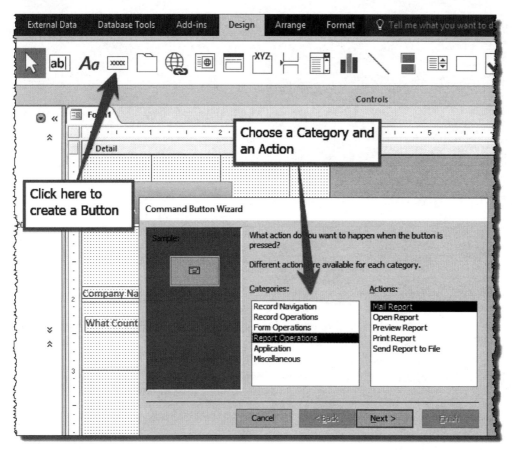

If you're experienced in writing macros or VBA code, this is an easy way to integrate that custom functionality into your Access form. If not, there are still numerous actions you can choose, via the wizard, that don't involve writing code.

Exercise: Adding list controls and command buttons

In this exercise, you'll add list controls and command buttons to a form.

Do This	How & Why
1. Add a field to the Mailing List table to use in a new form. a) In the Navigation pane's Tables node, right-click the Mailing List table, and choose **Design View**. b) Add a new field to the table of the **Long Text** data type, and name it `Greeting`. c) Save the new table definition. 2. Create a form based on the Mailing List table.	

Do This	How & Why
a) Click **View** to see the Mailing List table datasheet, and observe the new, blank column for Greeting.	
b) On the Create tab, click **Form** to create a form with bound controls and the Mailing List table set as the RecordSource.	
3. Configure properties for a text control.	
a) Click in the **Greeting** bound text box, and from the Design tab, open the **Property Sheet**.	You'll set a default value for the Greeting field.
b) On the Data tab of the Greeting control, enter a Default Value of `"Thanks for being part of the team, it's been a fantastic year!"`	Do include the quotation marks.
4. Convert the Text Box bound to the Country field to a List Box.	
a) Right-click on the **Country** Text Box, and choose **List Box** from the Change To menu.	The Greeting Text Box (and its label) should automatically be moved down so that it doesn't overlap the new control. This approach can help new users when entering records.
b) Run the form in Form view, and click **New**.	In the Records group. Notice that the default value we configured shows up in the Greeting Text Box.
5. View a list of choices for the List Box.	
a) Return to Design view.	You want to display a list of all the Country values that could be part of the Mailing List. This Mailing List table was built from the Customers, Employees, and Supplier tables. So, you'll need an SQL statement that gets all the unique Country values from all four tables (the original three plus Mailing List).
b) Click the **Country** List Box, and display the **Property Sheet**.	
c) Click on the property sheet **Data** tab, and click the **Row Source** property.	
d) Click the Row Source ⋯ button.	To bring up the query builder.
e) Close the Show Table window without adding any tables, and click **Union**.	In the Query Type group. The query builder switches to display a blank window for entering a SQL statement.

Do This	How & Why
f) Create an SQL statement that gets all the distinct Country values from all four tables by entering the following SQL code: `SELECT Country from Suppliers union Select Country from Employees union Select Country from Customers union Select Country from [Mailing List] order by Country`	Line breaks are not significant. The "union" statement automatically selects only distinct values.
g) Click **Run**.	To verify that you're getting a non-duplicated list of countries. There should be about 25 or 26 values (being off by one or two is fine).
h) Return to SQL View.	Click **View**.
i) Click **Close**, and click **Yes** to confirm saving the new statement as the Row Source property of the control.	
j) Run the form in Layout or Form view.	The previously configured Country value for each record should be selected in the List Box, indicating that the value from the underlying table is reflected.
6. Create a Print Mailing List command button for the Mailing List table.	
a) Return to Design view, and drag the bottom of the Form Footer bar down so that you can see grids.	We need some space to add controls.
b) On the Design tab, in the Controls gallery, click the **Button** control.	
c) Draw a Button near the left side of the Form Footer section.	The Control Wizard appears to help you configure the button's action.
d) Choose **Miscellaneous** from the Categories list, then click **Print Table** in the Actions list, then click **Next**.	
e) Select the **Mailing List** table from the list, then click **Next**.	You're provided with a choice of having a button with text or a button with an image.

Do This	How & Why
f) Leave the image as is, or choose **Text** and change the text to Print Mailing List; then click **Next**, and click **Finish**.	
g) In the Property Sheet for the button, click the **Event** tab.	The On Click event is set to [Embedded Macro], reflecting the results of your journey through the wizard.
h) Run the form in Form or Layout view, and click the button.	The table should display along with a print dialog.
i) If you have no printers configured (or don't wish to print) to print the table, cancel printing.	
j) Dismiss any error messages that may display.	Your purpose was to test the functionality of the button.
7. Save and close the form and the table.	

Changing the layout of controls

Selecting the best layout for a form's controls can make it easier for the user to navigate it and understand it. This is especially true if the form contains many fields.

1. In Design view, select one or more controls.
   - Right-click a control to display the context menu.
   - To select multiple controls, use the mouse to draw a rectangle that encloses the controls you wish to select, then right-click the selection to display the context menu.
2. Select the desired Layout options.
   - **Align** lines up controls by the left, right, top, or bottom. Choosing right, for example, aligns the right edge of all selected controls to the right edge of the far-right control.
   - **Size** resizes controls to the tallest or shortest of the selected controls or to the dots in the form's grid. Or, you can choose **To Fit** to size the control exactly as its displayed content. (This has more effect on labels and command buttons, for example. Text Box controls, by contrast, do not resize because of this choice in Design view, and they will not display any dynamic resizing behavior in Form view.)
   - **Position** provides two additional options: **Bring To Front** and **Send To Back**, to manage the stacking order of controls when parts of the controls inhabit the same form space. This option choice has no discernible effect if controls don't overlap.
3. Observe the Arrange tab.

   It contains the above layout options and many more. In addition, the Sizing and Spacing group contains other options, including those for changing horizontal and vertical spacing between controls.

Setting the tab order

Many users, including data entry professionals, enter or edit many records in one sitting. Providing a logical tab order for a form's controls enables users to efficiently and step through data entry in a logical sequence.

Although it's true that a user can easily focus on any enabled field by clicking it, data-entry people who value speed find that having to click on every destination field slows them down. Tabbing from field to field, instead of using the mouse, is far more efficient and expedient. Thus, the correct Tab Order setting is paramount.

By default, Access sets the tab order for each control you add to the form to one number higher than the previous control. For example, if the Text Box the user is working on has a Tab Order setting of 6, after pressing the Tab key, the cursor jumps to the control with its Tab Order set to 7.

This works well without any necessary intervention by you, provided that you lay out your controls in a top-to-bottom, left-to-right order, and that you've never repositioned them from their initial layout. Most often, however, form design involves a series of edits made over time. The Tab Order setting doesn't change dynamically. So, your job is to make sure that those settings are correct. Luckily, you don't have to go through each individual control's Tab Order setting in the Property Sheet to make this adjustment.

1. On the Design tab, click **Tab Order**.

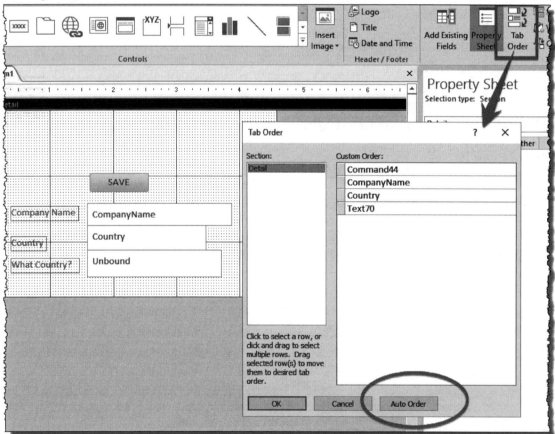

2. Choose the section of the form you're working on, then drag and drop the control names in the Custom Order box on the right.

   To make the job even easier, choose the **Auto Order** button to have Access align the controls in their currently situated order as it appears on the form. However, it's best to do all your alignment, positioning, and spacing work first, and then use Tab Order. In this way, you've not only made the form easy to look at, but efficient to use.

Exercise: Changing the layout of controls

In this exercise, you'll create a form, add controls, and then change their layout.

Do This	How & Why
1. Create a new form and add controls.	

a) Create a new blank form in Design view.	On the Create tab, click **Form Design**.
b) Set the RecordSource property of the form to the Invoices query.	On the Data tab of the Property Sheet, choose **Invoices** in the drop-down list.
c) Click **Add Existing Fields**.	In the Tools group.
d) Click the **ShipName** field, and drag it to the Detail section of the form.	
e) Widen the bound Text Box.	
f) Drag **OrderDate** onto the form the same way.	

Access 2016 Relational Database Design

Do This	How & Why
g) Drag five or six more fields onto the Detail section of the Form.	Leave them unaligned for the moment.
2. Align and resize the controls.	
a) Select all the new form controls, right-click the selection, and click **Align > Right**.	Use **Ctrl**+click to select each one, or use the mouse to drag a rectangle that encloses the controls.
b) Right-click the selection again, and click **Size > To Widest**.	All the Text Box controls should now be aligned and sized the same.
c) If you'd like to realign any of the controls, explore other Align, Size, and Position options, and drag the labels to align them vertically on the form.	Click and drag so that you select at least part of all the labels (but *not* the Text Boxes).
d) Repeat the Alignment and Sizing steps you used for the Text Boxes to line up the controls as you would like them displayed.	
3. Move controls and reset the tab order as you wish.	
a) Drag two or three of the textboxes to new positions, and realign them, as needed.	
b) Run the form in Form or Layout view, and use the Tab key to move through the fields.	Notice that you're jumping around in the order in which you originally added the fields, which doesn't suit the new arrangement. You'll need to fix that!
c) In Design view, click **Tab Order**; then click **Auto Order**, and click **OK**.	
d) Run the form again, and use the Tab key to navigate the form's controls.	You're now tabbing through them in the order in which the fields are currently aligned.
4. Save your changes, naming your form `Aligned Controls Form`, and close the form.	

Assessment: Form controls

1. Which of the following statements about form controls is *incorrect*?

   - The Use Control Wizards option is located in the Controls design gallery.
   - Layout view and Design view offer a wide variety of controls in the Design tab's Controls group.
   - Each control must have a unique name, which you must assign to it.
   - You can always change a control's size after the fact by selecting and resizing it.

2. True or False? When creating a List Box, when the number of choices exceeds the available space, scroll bars are automatically enabled by Access.

   - True
   - False

3. Which of the following statements is *incorrect*?

   - Using the List Box and Combo Box as bound controls requires setting their Row Source property.
   - A Combo Box is a drop-down box with a pre-configured list of choices, so it takes up less space than the other list controls.
   - An *Option Group* creates a set of buttons in which the user is permitted to pick exactly one.
   - With the List Box, users cannot add their own choices; however, you can manually change this default setting.

4. True or False? To add a command button to a form, you must manually create an underlying macro or write SQL statements.

   - True
   - False

5. Which of the following statements is *incorrect*?

   - Access sets the tab order for each control you add to the form to one number higher than the previous control.
   - After you've created a form, if you change the order of its controls, you must manually change the tab order of each control.
   - It's best to do all your alignment, positioning, and spacing work first, and then set the tab order.
   - Tabbing from field to field, instead of using the mouse, is far more efficient and expedient.

Summary: Forms

You should now know how to:

- Create simple forms, use different forms for different views, and create bound and unbound forms both from scratch and using the Form Wizard
- Design a form design, set and customize form properties, and work with form sections
- Use data-binding controls, understand the types of forms and their uses, and change the layout and tab order of form controls

Synthesis: Forms

In this synthesis exercise, you'll use the Form Wizard to create a form, and then lay out, add, and align controls.

1. Open the `FormsSynthesis DB` database.
   Form the current chapter folder, if necessary.
2. Create a form using the Form Wizard.
3. Include the following table fields:
   - Categories: **CategoryName**
   - Products: **ProductName**
   - Products: **SupplierID**
   - Products: **CategoryID**
   - Products: **Discontinued**
   - Suppliers: **CompanyName**
   - Suppliers: **ContactName**
   - Suppliers: **Country**
   - Suppliers: **Phone**

   If necessary, set the form to be viewed by Categories. When prompted, choose to view the form in Datasheet view, and name it `Product Categories`; keep the default subform name.

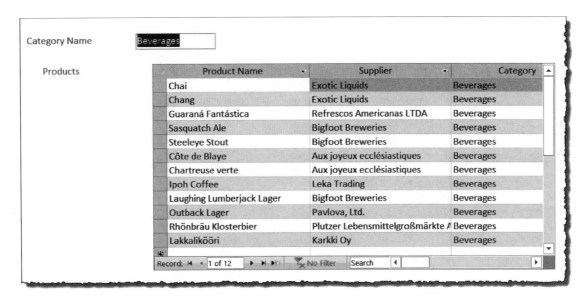

4. Filter the results to display only those suppliers located in the UK, Brazil, France, Singapore, and Finland.
5. Change the formatting and color of any controls you wish.
6. Change the layout, positions, and alignment of the form's controls.
7. Add a form header that displays whatever information you wish, but do include the date and time.
8. Add Preview, Mailing List, and Print Table command buttons to the form.
9. Use the query builder to create a query that displays product order totals by supplier.
   Add to the form whatever elements are necessary.
10. Add **OrderID** and **OrderDate** fields to your query.
11. Create a calculated field for the order date by entering the code string `DaysSinceOrder: DateDiff("d",[OrderDate],Date())`.
12. Hide the Discontinued field.
13. Change the layout, alignment, and formatting of your form's elements.
14. Set the tab order of your form's controls.
15. Name, save, and then close your query, as well as any other forms or tables you've opened.

Chapter 6: Reports

You will learn how to:

- Create reports and control data sources
- Add, move, and manipulate report controls
- Add images to and format reports

Module A: Creating Reports

Forms allow users to interact with the data: insert new records, edit, and delete. Reports are where you display that information, either on the screen or for printing. In this module, you'll explore the basics of creating an Access Report, and understand how to bind a report to a table or query.

You will learn how to:

- Create a simple report and control its properties
- Understand and control various data sources for reports
- Use the Report Wizard to quickly create reports

Report basics

If you've worked with Access forms, you'll see familiar functionality in reports. Like forms, reports also have controls, but keep in mind you're using these for display purposes instead of user interaction. You could still use a control like a List Box or Combo Box, but it's just not as common since those controls are typically used to simplify user input.

Since you will usually create reports in a business scenario to make sense of the data, you will also make extensive use of grouping and summarizing, much more than you do in Forms. If you want to know how, for example, much each of customer has spent over the last year, it's far easier and has greater impact to see this in summary form. Reports are an ideal place to display that kind of information.

Report views

In the process of designing the report, you'll have four views available. Like forms, reports have *Layout view* that gives you the most possible flexibility. In Layout view the report is actually running, but you have the ability to edit controls either visually or through their property sheets. Almost all your design work can be done in Layout view. What's really nice here is that, especially for text fields of varying lengths, the report is actually running, so you can adjust Text Box control heights and widths based on actual data you're seeing instead of guessing at it in Design view.

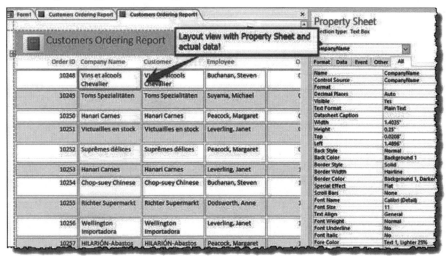

You can probably get a better idea about the "bones" of your report in Design view. You can get there by clicking **View** > **Design View**. Design view seems to be a more intuitive way to adjust settings around headers and footers, since reports can contain these sections not only for pages, but for custom groupings as well. There are also some controls you can't add in Layout view that are available here, as well as some items in the Property Sheet.

Chapter 6: Reports / Module A: Creating Reports

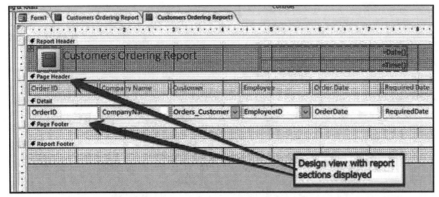

The other two views allow you to see the finished report. Report View shows how it will display on screen, and Print Preview is a full-featured look at the printed report document, including buttons to allow the user to adjust the report orientation, columns, and margins, as well as to export the report to Excel, a PDF, a text file and other common formats and applications.

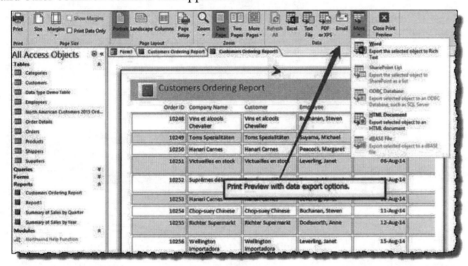

Exercise: Creating a basic products report

In this exercise, you will create a simple products report that displays products information, change some of its properties, and use different report views.

Do This	How & Why
1. Open `CreatingReportsDB`.	From the current chapter folder.
2. Create a quick report.	
a) Open the Products table in Datasheet view.	
b) On the Create tab, click **Report**.	A new report opens in Layout view. Notice that you have a running report with live data, and a property sheet to configure report elements.
3. Make the Supplier column stand out.	
a) Click any cell in the Supplier column.	

Do This	How & Why
b) Use the Property Sheet to add a Back Color.	Click the Format tab of the Properties sheet, and in the Back Color box, select **Background Light Header**.
c) Change the Font Weight to **Semi-Bold**.	
d) Change the Fore Color to a red.	Click the ellipsis to select from a color palette.

4. Change the image in the report header.

   a) Switch to Design view.

   b) Select the image icon in the header.

   c) Change the Picture Type property to **Linked**.

   You'll link to an external image

   d) Use the `Report.png` image as the Picture property.

   Click the ellipsis next to the Picture property, select the image file, and click **Open**.

   e) Change the Size Mode property to **Stretch**.

   f) Resize the image by dragging a corner.

   Don't make it too big.

5. Print preview the report.

   a) Click **View > Print Preview**.

   You can see how the report will print. You can use the navigation buttons at the bottom of the preview to move through the pages.

   b) Click **Two Pages**.

   To view two pages at a time. The report is wide enough that it needs two pages just to fit.

   c) Click **Size > Legal**.

   d) Click **Landscape**.

   This is starting to look better. You could adjust the column sizes to try to get all the columns on one page.

6. Save the report as `Basic Products Report`.

   Click **Save**, enter the name, then click **OK**.

7. Close the report and the Products table.

Data sources

Your first job with the report is to decide what data to show, and that's simply a matter of setting up the *Record Source*. The Record Source can be any existing table or query, or you can create a custom SQL statement. All the tables and queries in your database will be listed in the drop-down box for the Report Source property in the Report's property sheet.

The Report object also has Filter and Order By properties that show on the Data tab of the Property Sheet.

Setting up data sources

There are a couple of ways to set up data sources.

- To use a table or query as a data source, click the drop-down for the Report Source property in the Report's property sheet.
    All database tables and queries will be listed here.
- To design a custom SQL statement, click the ellipsis (…) on the right of the Record Source property to open the Query Builder. This window looks and functions exactly like query Design View.

If you need to modify the Report's data source at any time, return to the Query Builder. Common reasons to do this might be the need to add another table (to show related data you missed the first time around), or to create a new calculated field that didn't exist in the original table or query. If you change a custom SQL statement, no other Access objects are affected. If you change an existing query, the query itself is changed, so take care that you don't negatively impact other objects that might depend on the query's current configuration.

When you finish with the Query Builder, you'll see a custom SQL statement or the name of a table or query in the Report Source property. As you'd expect, the report is created dynamically, in that the data you display in Report or Print Preview view is a snapshot of the data at the time the report was run. In order to have the most current data, run the report again, and Access automatically executes the underlying SQL statement.

Filtering and ordering reports

Filtering modifies which records are shown in a report. Ordering controls the order in which results appear.

- You can set a *Filter* that chooses a subset of records returned by the Record Source. If you had a report that showed your customers' order information but you wanted to see information from 2016, you could set the Filter to `Year([OrderDate])=2016`. To create a more complex expression using multiple fields, just add the appropriate operator into the expression. To see order information from 2016 for only Canadian customers, change the Filter to `Year([OrderDate])=2016 and [Country]="Canada"`. There is a Filter On Load property you can set to **Yes** to cause the filter to be automatically applied when the report opens. Whatever value you use, the person viewing the report can click **Toggle Filter** button to either apply or eliminate the filter (if they have access to the ribbon).
- The *Order By property* also uses a field name or names from the Report Source. Ascending sort is the default when you specify a field, so numeric values will be sorted lowest to highest, text from A to Z, and dates from earliest to latest. To sort in the reverse direction, add **DESC** (for descending) after the field name. To sort by multiple fields, separate each field expression with a comma. Access sorts by the field names in order. The example shows a report that is filtered by a year and by Ship City, and then ordering by Ship City in ascending order and by Extended Price in descending order. There is also an Order By On Load property that works the same way as the Filter On Load property.

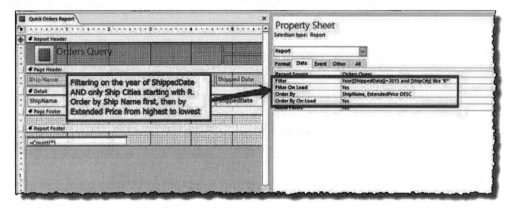

And this is that filtered, ordered report.

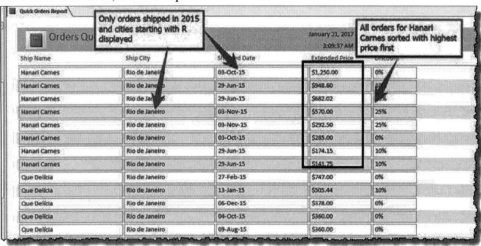

Exercise: Controlling a report's data source

In this exercise, you'll set the data source for a report and then filter and order it.

Do This	How & Why
1. View the results for Calculated Query.	It is in the list of queries for the database. The results include the name of the month in which a product was ordered, as well as a ReorderStatus field indicating whether the product needs to be reordered.
2. Create the record source for a new report.	
a) On the Create tab, click **Report Design**.	To display a new, blank report.
b) Display the property sheet for the report.	If necessary.
c) Display the Select Table window for the Record Source property.	On the Data tab of the property sheet, click the ellipsis next to Record Source. From here you could create your own query to use as the Record Source. We will use a pre-existing query, but it's good to know you can build this yourself if needed.

Do This	How & Why
d) Close the **Show Table** window.	
e) Click the Close button on the right of the ribbon.	
3. Specify Calculated Query as the Report Source.	From the Record Source drop-down, select **Calculated Query**.
4. Add controls to the report as shown.	
a) Click **Add Existing Fields** on the Report Design Tools Design tab.	To display a field list.
b) Drag the **Month Ordered** field into the Detail section.	Drop it near the middle of the second grid block from the left, near the top.

c) Drag each other report field to the detail section.

To look approximately like this (Exact positioning isn't that important).

d) Drag the Page Footer section up to just below the bottom of the fields you've added.	If necessary.
5. View the report.	Click **View**. You should have live data with alternating color bands to separate each record.
6. Save the report as `Product Orders Report`.	
7. Filter and order the report.	
a) Change to Design View and display the property sheet.	If necessary, select **Report** from the Selection Type list.
b) Set the Filter value to `[Month Ordered]="April"`.	To show only records ordered in the month of April.
c) Set the Order By value to `[ProductName]`.	To sort by Product Name.
d) Set the Filter On Load property to **Yes**.	To cause the filter to be applied whenever the report is run.

Do This	How & Why
e) Set the Order By On Load property to **Yes**.	To cause the report to be ordered whenever it is run.
8. Save and close, then run the report.	You can run the report by double-clicking it in the Objects pane. If you entered Filter and Order By information correctly, you should see only products from April, and they should be in alphabetical order by product.
9. Close all open objects and the database.	

Automatic report generators

Access provides a couple of quick ways to generate reports automatically.

- If you have a table or query open, click the **Report** button on the Create tab of the ribbon to create a report with that table or query set as the Report Source. It's a good starting point, and everything is editable.
- The Report Wizard can guide you, step-by-step, though the process of creating a report.

Using the Report Wizard

You can use the Report Wizard to generate a report from any existing table or query, or you can create a new report source by choosing two or more related tables or queries.

1. On the Create tab, in the Reports group, click **Report Wizard**.
2. Select a data source and fields.
    Use the drop-down to select a table or query, then double-click fields to move them to the Selected Fields list. Here, you're choosing to see the FirstName and LastName fields from the Employees table. You can select fields from multiple sources; just keep selecting different tables or queries and moving their fields into the list.

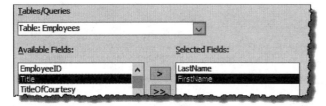

3. Click **Next** and choose how to view the report.
    You can have it summarized based on various field choices you've made.

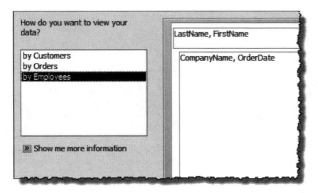

4. Click **Next** and decide on any grouping for the report.

   Here, orders will be grouped by company. You can add more levels of grouping if needed.

5. Click **Next** and decide on ordering.

   This report will be ordered by OrderDate, with the latest first (descending order).

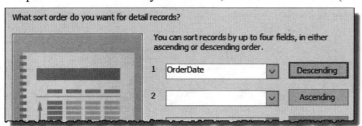

6. Click **Next** and select a layout for the report.

   Consider using the Landscape orientation when you have a large number of fields. You'll still probably have some layout work to do after you open the report, though. You can choose to have the Wizard adjust the field widths, but the widths you're forcing it to create may not show all the data you need people to see.

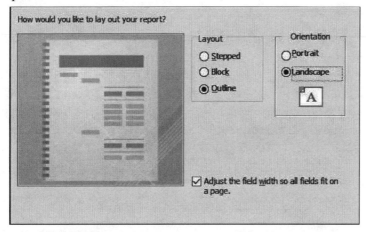

7. Click **Next** and enter a title for the report.
8. Click **Finish** to view the report.

Here's what this sample finished report looks like. You'd have some more work to do to make this pretty, but as far as the accuracy of the data and solving the business problem, this was a quick solution.

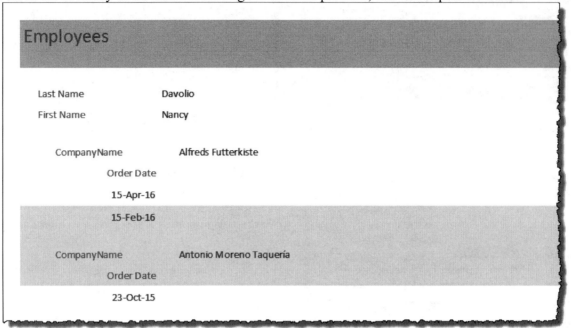

Exercise: Creating a report using the Report Wizard

In this exercise, you'll use the Report Wizard to create a report that gives product and supplier information by category.

Do This	How & Why
1. Start a new report using the Report Wizard.	On the Create tab, in the Reports group, click **Report Wizard**. The first step of the Report Wizard appears, allowing you to select data sources and fields to include.
2. Select these fields from the Categories table: • Category Name • Description	In the Tables/Queries list, click **Table: Categories**. Then double-click each field to move it to the Selected Fields list.
3. Select these fields from the Products table: • Product Name • UnitsInStock • UnitPrice	Select the table, then double-click the fields.
4. Select these fields from the Suppliers table: • Company Name • Country	The Selected Fields list should look like this. Selected Fields: CategoryName Description ProductName UnitsInStock UnitPrice CompanyName Country

Do This	How & Why
5. Click **Next** and click **by Categories**.	To view the report first by category.
6. Click **Next** and double-click **Product Name**.	To group the report by Product Name. CategoryName, Description **ProductName** UnitsInStock, UnitPrice, CompanyName, Country
7. Click **Next** and sort by Company Name.	Select **Company Name** in the first sort ordering box.
8. Click **Next** and click **Block**.	To select a layout for the report.
9. Click **Next** and name the report.	Name it **Products by Category**.
10. Click **Finish** to preview the report.	The Wizard creates a fully formatted report for you with very little trouble. It might not be perfect, but you can at least use the Wizard as a starting point for many or most reports.
11. Close the report.	
12. Close the database.	

A report generated by the Report Wizard

Products by Category

Category	Description	ProductName	Company Name	n Stock	Unit Price
Beverage	Soft drinks, coffees, teas, beers, and ales	Chai	Exotic Liquids	39	$18.00
		Chang	Exotic Liquids	17	$19.00
		Chartreuse verte	Aux joyeux ecclésiastiqu	69	$18.00
		Côte de Blaye	Aux joyeux ecclésiastiqu	17	$263.50
		Guaraná Fantástic	Refrescos Americanas LT	20	$4.50
		Ipoh Coffee	Leka Trading	17	$46.00
		Lakkalikööri	Karkki Oy	57	$18.00
		Laughing Lumberja	Bigfoot Breweries	52	$14.00
		Outback Lager	Pavlova, Ltd.	15	$15.00
		Rhönbräu Klosterb	Plutzer Lebensmittelgro	125	$7.75
		Sasquatch Ale	Bigfoot Breweries	111	$14.00
		Steeleye Stout	Bigfoot Breweries	20	$18.00
Condime	Sweet and savory sauces, relishes, spreads, and seasonings	Aniseed Syrup	Exotic Liquids	13	$10.00
		Chef Anton's Cajun	New Orleans Cajun Delig	53	$22.00

Assessment: Creating reports

1. In which report views can you make design changes to a report? Select all correct answers.
   - Report view
   - Print Preview
   - Layout view
   - Design view

2. Which of the following are ways to specify data sources for a report? Select all correct answers.
   - Automatically using the Report button with a table open.
   - By using the Report Wizard.
   - By using the Expression Builder for a report's Data Source property.

3. Which of the following approaches could you use to see only a subset of records from a table in a report?
   - Use the report's Order By property.
   - Use the report's Filter property.
   - Base the report on a query.
   - Show only certain fields in the report.

4. The Report Wizard is quick, but does not allow you to group data in a report. True or false?
   - True
   - False

Module B: Report controls

Report controls are the tools you use to display information on reports. They work much like form controls, but some serve different purposes. Report controls can show field data, static text, summary information, and graphics.

You will learn how to:

- Add and position controls in a report
- User report sections
- Add calculated fields to a report
- Group and summarize report data

Adding report controls

Report controls can be added to display fields from individual records, or to show summaries by grouped report section. You can do this in either Layout or Design view, though not all the controls are available in Layout view. Controls can be added in a few different ways.

- In the Controls group of the Design tab, click the control you want. Then drag your mouse in a report section to draw the control and an associated label.
- Display the Field List window and then double-click a field name or drag it into the form in the appropriate section. The control in this case will automatically be data-bound with its Control Source property set to the field that you chose.

Positioning report controls

Labels move with their associated control when you reposition the control. You're also free to change the label text at any time. Changes to the field's Caption property will not automatically be reflected in the label's text. If you select and delete the control, the associated label will be deleted as well.

In Design view, you can select multiple controls by drawing a rectangle around them with the mouse. Any control that's partially or fully enclosed by the drawn box will be selected. Then right-click in any of the selected controls to access Layout options for the group. Here are some ideas for positioning controls.

- Use **Align** options to line up controls by the left, right, top or bottom. Select **Right**, for example, will line up the right edges of all selected controls to the right edge of the farthest-right control.
- Use **Size** options to re-size controls to the tallest or shortest of the selected controls, to the dots in the form's grid, or to be exactly as big as its displayed content (use **To Fit** for this). This last option has more effect on labels and command buttons. Text Box controls by contrast will not resize because of this choice in Design view, and will not display any dynamic resizing behavior in Form view.
- **Position** gives you two options, **Bring To Front** and **Send To Back**, to manage the stacking order of controls when parts of the controls inhabit the same form space. These options have no discernible effect if there's no control overlap, and given that we're formatting here for screen or print, it's relatively uncommon to overlap controls at all.
- The Arrange tab has some more sophisticated options, including options for changing the spacing between controls, increasing or decreasing horizontal or vertical space, and making the spacing equal in one or the other dimension.

Placing controls in report sections

It's useful to think from the inside out, from the display of one record, all the way out to doing calculations and summaries for groups, and then totaling for an entire report. What shows up where is going to be based on your creation of sections and placing the right controls in each section.

The section where individual record information appears is the Detail section. You can choose to place labels here, but more often you would place those in one of the header sections, either at the page or group level. Here's the default layout for a report created by a simple click of the Report button with the Employees table open.

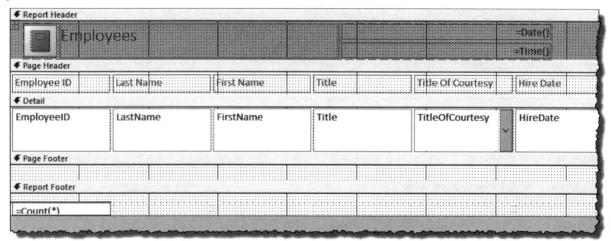

There are Report Header and Report Footer sections, each of which will only show up once, at the beginning and ending of the report. By default, the Report button and the Report Wizard both add a calculated field showing the total number of records in the report (Not including summary rows) in the Report Footer. The SQL expression Count(*) creates that value. You can safely delete this control if it's not useful for you.

The Page Header and Page Footer sections will show up once at the top and bottom of each page, in both Print Preview and Report view.

All report sections have a `Display When` property that's initially set to **Always**. If there are sections you want to change this for, set the property to **Screen Only** or **Print Only**.

Exercise: Manipulating controls in a report

In this exercise, you'll improve the look of a report by adding controls and manipulating their position and appearance.

Do This	How & Why
1. Open the `ControllingReportsDB` database.	In the current chapter folder.
2. Open **Product Suppliers for Controls**.	
3. Switch to Layout view.	This is the view you'll use to work with the report.

Do This	How & Why
4. Display the property sheet for the report.	On the Design tab, click Property Sheet, then select Report from the property sheet's drop-down. 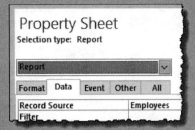
5. Add the Picture field to the report.	
a) Display the query builder for the report.	Click the ellipsis (…) next to the Record Source property.
b) In the Categories table, double-click **Picture**.	To add the field to the query that serves as the Record Source for the report.
c) Close and save the query.	Click the Close button at the right of the Query Tools Design tab, then click **Yes** to save changes to the query. You've added a new field to the report data, but there's no control to show it yet.
6. Place a control to show the Picture field.	
a) Switch to Design view.	
b) Make the CategoryID Header section taller.	Drag its bottom border down to make room for the picture you're going to place here.
c) Click **Add Existing Fields**.	On the Design tab.
d) Drag the Picture Field into the CategoryID Header section of the report.	
e) Delete the label for the field, then size it as shown.	Delete only the label, not the Bound Object Frame control. 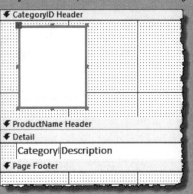

Do This	How & Why
7. Switch to Report view.	The category name is showing on every line item. We'd like to see this only once per category.
8. Move the Category Name and Description controls.	
a) Switch to Design view.	
b) Move the controls as shown.	You can drag them or cut and paste them to move them from the detail section to the CategoryID Header. A selected control can be moved within a section by using the arrow keys.
c) View the report.	Now the category information appears only once for each category.
9. Change the appearance of the CategoryID Header section.	
a) Change the Fill/Back Color to a light color.	In Design view, right-click within the CategoryID Header section, click the Fill/Back Color arrow, and select a color.
b) Select both the Category Name and Description controls.	Click one, then hold **Ctrl** and click the other. If you look at the property sheet now, it says "multiple selection."
c) Set Back Style to **Transparent**.	
d) Set Font Size to **14**.	
e) Set Font Weight to **Semi-Bold**.	
f) Widen the Description control.	Click to deselect both controls, then select and size the Description control.
g) View the report.	If the Description control still isn't wide enough, go back to Design view and fix it.

Do This	How & Why
10. Improve the layout of the controls of the report. • In the Page Header, delete the Category label and the Description label. • In the Detail, drag Product Name to the left and widen it. • Use Layout view to manipulate controls to your liking. 11. Save the report.	Compare your results to the sample after the exercise.

Products by Category

ProductName	Company Name	Units In Stock	Unit Price
Beverages Soft drinks, coffees, teas, beers, and ales			
Chai	Exotic Liquids	39	$18.00
Chang	Exotic Liquids	17	$19.00
Chartreuse verte	Aux joyeux ecclésiastiqu	69	$18.00
Côte de Blaye	Aux joyeux ecclésiastiqu	17	$263.50
Guaraná Fantástica	Refrescos Americanas LT	20	$4.50
Ipoh Coffee	Leka Trading	17	$46.00
Lakkalikööri	Karkki Oy	57	$18.00
Laughing Lumberjack Lager	Bigfoot Breweries	52	$14.00
Outback Lager	Pavlova, Ltd.	15	$15.00
Rhönbräu Klosterbier	Plutzer Lebensmittelgro	125	$7.75
Sasquatch Ale	Bigfoot Breweries	111	$14.00
Steeleye Stout	Bigfoot Breweries	20	$18.00

Calculated fields

Because reports derive much of their benefit from the ability to summarize and group data, calculated fields are essential to their functionality. You'll probably find yourself wanting to create totals, calculate averages, show maximums and minimums, do statistical analysis, or many other common tasks.

Creating calculated fields

You create calculated fields by creating expressions within the Control Source property for a Text Box control.

1. Create a Text Box control to display the data you want.
2. In the control's Control Source property, click the ellipsis (…) to open the Expression Builder.
3. Pick an expression element (such as a function), then a category, then a value. For example, the Count(*) expression you've seen appears in the Functions>Built-in Functions>SQL Aggregate category.
4. Double-click a function name (or other value) to insert it in the top of the window, with a placeholder in the form of <<placeholder>>.

    Click the link on the bottom of the window to get more information about what type of data the function requires. In this case, <<expression>> is the name of a field on which to calculate an average with the Avg function.

    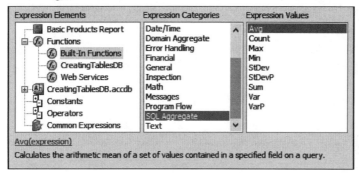

5. Replace all placeholders with appropriate values depending on the function.

    Here, the function needed a field name. By going back to the Expression Elements box and selecting the report, a list of field names appears in the middle box. You can then select the placeholder in the top window, then double-click the field name to add it to the calculated field expression.

    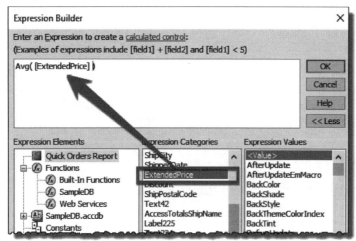

6. Click **OK** when the expression is complete.

After you've created an expression in the Control Source property, the value the control shows will depend on where it's placed. If it's in the Report Footer, for example, you'll an average of all the Extended Price detail records in the report.

Exercise: Creating a calculated field

You must have completed the preceding exercise, "Manipulating controls in a report," in order to do this one.

In this exercise, you'll add a field to the report to calculated the inventory total for each product.

Do This	How & Why
1. Open **Product Suppliers for Controls**.	If necessary. This is the same report you worked on in the previous exercise.
2. Add a label and a text box for a calculated field.	
a) Switch to Design view.	
b) Widen the report.	Drag its right edge to give you more room for new controls. This might not be necessary.
c) In the Details section, add a Text Box control to the right of Unit Price.	
d) Delete the label for the new Text Box control.	
e) Add a Label control in the Page Header section.	
f) Add the text `Inventory Total` to the Label.	

Do This	How & Why
g) Left Align the new Text Box and Label.	The new controls should look like this.
3. Display the property sheet for the new Text Box.	Select it, then click **Property Sheet**.
4. Create a calculated Control Source for the Text Box.	
a) Display the Expression Builder for the Control Source property.	On the property sheet's Data tab, click the ellipsis (…) next to the Control Source property.
b) Type `[UnitPrice]*[UnitsInStock]`.	This expression will calculate the total amount for the inventory of each product.
c) Click **OK**.	
5. Format the Text Box as **Currency**.	On the Format tab of the property sheet, change the Format property.
6. View the report.	Check the match on a couple of the inventory totals to see if the calculation is working.
7. Save the report.	

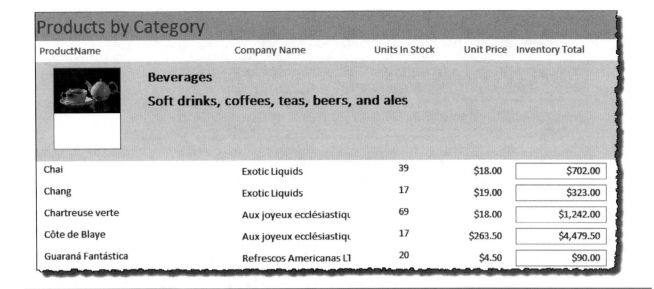

Grouping and summarizing

Sometimes calculations for an entire report aren't focused enough and you want data about a particular group in the report. For example, though it might be nice to know a company's average order price, you might also want to know the average order price per customer.

Access allows you to show both. If you have a report total calculation, you could simply copy that control into a Group Header or Group Footer section to get the calculation result for that group.

1. First create a group. Right-click the report and click **Sorting and Grouping** to display the Sorting and Grouping window at the bottom of the report.
2. Next, click **Add group** to select the fields you want to group on.
   In this example, using Ship Name will make it possible to get a calculation summary for each separate Ship Name.

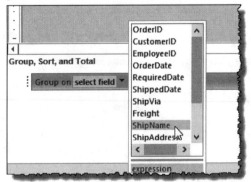

3. Add a text box control to the group header or footer and enter an expression in its Control Source property.
   In the example you've seen, you could simply copy the calculated field for the report average to the Ship Name Header or Footer section (or both). The placement of the control in this section will automatically restrict the calculation to only orders for this Ship Name. Here, there is a bound Text Box control in the section with its Control Source property set to Ship Name to complete the display.

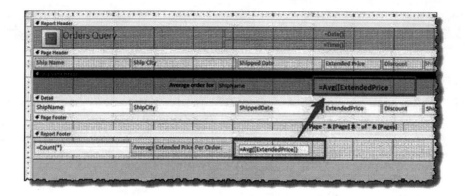

The following report shows the average order for each customer at the top of their section.

You have additional options available for configuring the display of the header or the footer, and whether to keep sections together on a page. Click **More** in the sorting and grouping window.

Exercise: Grouping a report and adding a group summary calculation

You must have completed the previous exercise, "Creating a calculated field," in order to complete this one.

In this exercise, you'll add a group footer, then add a summary calculation to a Text Box to show total inventory by category.

Do This	How & Why
1. Open Product Supplier for Controls in Design view.	If necessary.
2. Create a CategoryID Footer section.	
a) Right-click the report, then click **Sorting and Grouping**.	To display the Group, Sort, and Total area at the bottom of the report.

Do This	How & Why
b) Click **More** > **without a footer section** > **with a footer section**.	The More button is next to "Group on CategoryID." 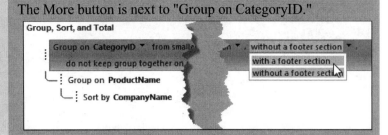 There is now a CategoryID Footer section in the report.
3. Add a Text Box control to the CategoryID Footer section. a) Widen the section if you need more room. b) Click the Text Box control, and draw the control. c) Align the Text Box with the Inventory Total text box in the Detail section. d) For the label text, enter `Inventory Total for Category`.	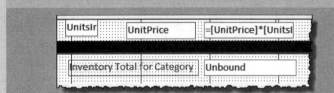
4. Enter the calculation for the new Text Box.	
a) Display the Expression Builder for the Text Box's Control Source property.	Display the property sheet and click the ellipsis (…).
b) Enter `Sum([UnitPrice]*[UnitsInStock])`.	This expression calculates the sum of all the totals for the category.
c) Click **OK**.	
d) Format the control as **Currency**.	On the Format tab, change the Format property.
5. Save and then run the report.	
6. Close the report.	
7. Close the database.	

Products by Category

ProductName	Company Name	Units In Stock	Unit Price	Inventory Total
Beverages				
Soft drinks, coffees, teas, beers, and ales				
Chai	Exotic Liquids	39	$18.00	$702.00
Chang	Exotic Liquids	17	$19.00	$323.00
Chartreuse verte	Aux joyeux ecclésiastiqu	69	$18.00	$1,242.00
Côte de Blaye	Aux joyeux ecclésiastiqu	17	$263.50	$4,479.50
Guaraná Fantástica	Refrescos Americanas LT	20	$4.50	$90.00
Ipoh Coffee	Leka Trading	17	$46.00	$782.00
Lakkalikööri	Karkki Oy	57	$18.00	$1,026.00
Laughing Lumberjack Lager	Bigfoot Breweries	52	$14.00	$728.00
Outback Lager	Pavlova, Ltd.	15	$15.00	$225.00
Rhönbräu Klosterbier	Plutzer Lebensmittelgro	125	$7.75	$968.75
Sasquatch Ale	Bigfoot Breweries	111	$14.00	$1,554.00
Steeleye Stout	Bigfoot Breweries	20	$18.00	$360.00
			Inventory Total for Category	$12,480.25

Assessment: Report controls

1. What is the best way to ensure that a label in a report header lines up with its associated information in the detail section? Select the one best answer.

    - Use Size options.
    - Use Position options.
    - Use Align options.

2. Which report sections shows once for each group of data in a report? Select the one best answer.

    - Page sections.
    - Category sections.
    - Detail section.

3. Calculated fields are useful on in grouped and summary sections of a report. True or false?

    - True
    - False

4. You do not need to remember field names when using the Expression Builder. True or false?

    - True
    - False

5. You can group by only one field in a report. True or false?

    - True
    - False

Module C: Formatting reports

You have enormous control over the formatting of reports to make them look and print just the way you want. You can control page layout options, add images, and use themes, among other options.

You will learn how to:

- Control report Page Setup options
- Insert data-bound and static images in reports
- User and customize themes

Report Page Setup options

You can use options on the Report Design Tools Page Setup tab to control various aspects of how the report will appear. For example, reports can be oriented in either Landscape (wider) or Portrait (higher).

You can also control margins on this tab. Click **Margins** and select one of three built-in margin settings. If you'd like more controls, click **Page Setup** to display the Page Setup window, where you can individually set each margin.

You can also present a report in multiple columns. Click **Columns** to display the Columns tab in the Page Setup window, where you can set the number of columns, as well as the spacing between the rows and between columns.

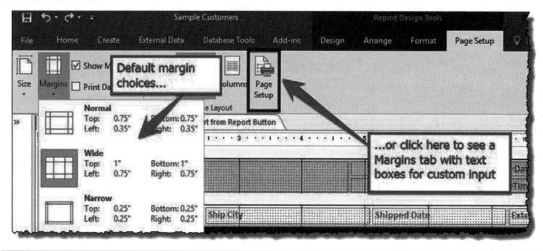

Images and other objects

Images in reports fall into two categories: those that will change because they're bound to data, usually in the Detail section; and static images like a company logo or an icon that focuses attention on a particular field. Each type requires a different control.

Images from a database

If a control gets data from your tables or queries, it does so because you've set its Control Source property. The way you display an image from your tables works the same way as how you display text controls information. The difference is that you will need to use a Bound Object Frame control. Place the control in the section you want, and set the Control Source property to the field that holds the image.

You should also set the Size Mode property. The default value is **Zoom**, which means Access will display the entire picture with its actual aspect ratio, and it may not fill up the entire frame. The **Clip** value will show the upper left corner of the image, with the original aspect ratio, but only as much as fits in the frame. The **Stretch** value often has unflattering results, but it does fill the entire frame at the expense of losing the original image's aspect ratio.

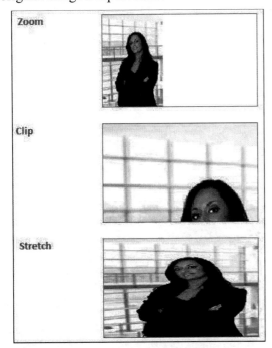

Static images and other objects

There are two controls you can use to show a static image (one that's not stored in your database): the Image control and the Unbound Object Frame.

The Image control displays any image you want from the file system. The Unbound Object Frame control, on the other hand, can display a wide variety of OLE objects. OLE stands for "Object Linking and Embedding," a Microsoft technology that lets you view (and edit) objects from one application inside another. So, within Access forms or reports, you could display or edit a Word document, Excel spreadsheet, Adobe Acrobat document, and many more object types. As long as the OLE "plumbing" for that particular application is set up on your machine, you're good to go.

This example shows both kinds of controls.

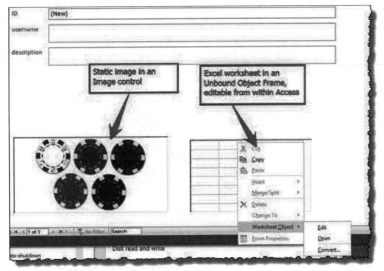

Users can edit an Unbound Object Frame control in a form, but in reports you'll mostly just display various objects types, like charts or graphs. The process for creating the control is the same though.

If you're simply looking to display an image, the easiest way to do it is to use an Image control. The Image control loads faster than the Unbound Object Frame (because there's less overhead in getting that done). Because reports are for viewing rather than editing, default to using the Image control for pictures, and keep the Unbound Object Frame handy for displaying any other type of object that's not stored in your database.

Exercise: Formatting reports and images

In this exercise, you'll experiment with image formatting and Page Layout options for a categorized products report.

Do This	How & Why
1. Open `FormattingReportsDB`.	
2. Open **Product Suppliers for Formatting**.	This report is in the CreatingReportsDB database located in the current chapter folder.
3. Improve the layout of the picture in the CategoryID Header.	
a) Switch to Design view.	
b) Change the Size Mode property for the picture to **Stretch**.	The Size Mode property is on the Format tab of the control's property sheet.
c) View the report.	Better. Now the picture is using the full area of its frame. But the aspect ratio is off.
4. Try some of these properties for the picture: • Back Style: **Transparent** • Border Width: **3 pt** • Border Color: a bright color • Special Effect: **Raised**	You can experiment to find formats you like.
5. Change the report orientation to **Landscape**.	On the Report Layout Tools Page Setup tab, click **Landscape**.
6. Experiment with Margin options.	These are also on the Page Setup tab.
7. Print Preview the report.	Click **View > Print Preview**. If you get a warning about the report being too wide to print, you might need to move fields around to compact the size, or choose a different paper size from the Size button on the Page Setup tab.
8. Save the report.	

Products by Category

ProductName	Company Name	Units In Stock	Unit Price	Inventory Total

Beverages
Soft drinks, coffees, teas, beers, and ales

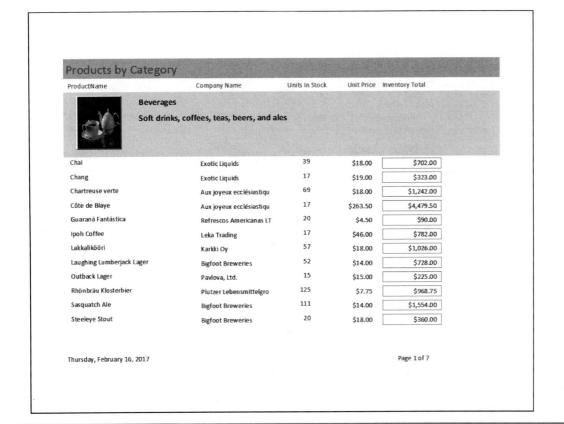

ProductName	Company Name	Units In Stock	Unit Price	Inventory Total
Chai	Exotic Liquids	39	$18.00	$702.00
Chang	Exotic Liquids	17	$19.00	$323.00
Chartreuse verte	Aux joyeux ecclésiastiqu	69	$18.00	$1,242.00
Côte de Blaye	Aux joyeux ecclésiastiqu	17	$263.50	$4,479.50
Guaraná Fantástica	Refrescos Americanas LT	20	$4.50	$90.00
Ipoh Coffee	Leka Trading	17	$46.00	$782.00
Lakkalikööri	Karkki Oy	57	$18.00	$1,026.00
Laughing Lumberjack Lager	Bigfoot Breweries	52	$14.00	$728.00
Outback Lager	Pavlova, Ltd.	15	$15.00	$225.00
Rhönbräu Klosterbier	Plutzer Lebensmittelgro	125	$7.75	$968.75
Sasquatch Ale	Bigfoot Breweries	111	$14.00	$1,554.00
Steeleye Stout	Bigfoot Breweries	20	$18.00	$360.00

Thursday, February 16, 2017   Page 1 of 7

Themes

Themes are a way to get a consistent look and feel throughout all the reports (and forms) in your database. Although you access theme settings in an individual report or form, you're actually setting the theme for the entire database.

Setting themes

The Theme button is on the Design tab. There are several themes available, and when you choose one, the report you have open will automatically change to show you a sample of what it looks like. A theme affects the colors and fonts of reports. You can also change each of those aspects individually, and save those customizations as your own theme.

If these themes look familiar, it might be because they're common to all Microsoft Office apps, making it easier to do some design branding across apps with a well-thought-out system of colors and fonts.

1. On the Design tab, click **Theme**.

    The Theme palette appears, giving you choices of themes.

    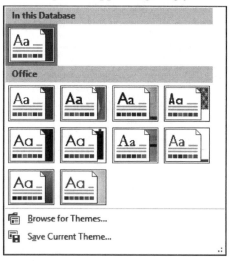

2. At this point you have choices.

    - Click a theme to apply it to the entire database.
    - Right-click a theme and choose to apply the theme to only the current report (**This Object Only**) or to all reports (**All Matching Objects**).

        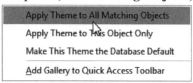

Exercise: Working with themes

You must have completed the previous exercise, Formatting reports and images, in order to complete this one.

In this exercise, you'll change some formatting, create a theme based on those changes, and then apply that custom theme to a new report.

Do This	How & Why
1. Open Product Suppliers for Formatting in Design view.	
2. Change the theme font for the report.	On the Design tab, In the Themes group, click **Font** and then select a font you like.
3. Change the theme color for the report.	Click the **Colors** button in the Themes group and choose a color group.
4. Save your settings as a custom theme.	
a) Click **Themes > Save Current Theme**.	To open the Save Current Theme window. Notice the default location where Office saves the theme, likely in a path ending in ...\Templates\Document Themes. This is important, because it will allow all your other Office apps to use the custom theme.
b) Save the theme as `Report Exercise Theme`.	
5. Save and close the report.	
6. Create a quick report.	It can be based on any table or query. Select one, then click **Report** on the Create tab.
7. Try applying various themes to the report.	
8. Apply the custom theme to the report.	In the Themes palette, select the custom theme. If you don't see a custom theme, you can click Browse For Themes and then navigate to and select the saved theme.
9. Close the report without saving it.	
10. Close all open objects and the database.	

Assessment: Formatting reports

1. Which of the following are Page Setup options for a report? Select all correct answers.

    - Margins
    - Data Source
    - Size
    - Page Layout
    - Background Image

2. Images in a report do not have to come from your database. True or false?

    - True
    - False

3. Which Size Mode setting is most appropriate if you want to be sure that an entire image shows and is not distorted? Select the one best answer.

    - Zoom
    - Clip
    - Stretch

4. Which control type do you use to display images that come from your database? Select the one best answer.

    - Image
    - Unbound Object Frame
    - Bound Object Frame

5. You can customize themes and save your customizations for future use. True or false?

    - True
    - False

Summary: Reports

In this chapter, you learned how to:

- Create reports, use report views, set up data sources, filter reports, order reports, and use the Report Wizard to quickly create a report
- Add, reposition, and reformat report controls; create calculated fields; and group and summarize data in a report
- Control report Page Setup options such as orientation and margins, control the appearance of images in a report, and use themes to quickly apply consistent formatting across reports and database objects

Synthesis: Reports

In this synthesis exercise, you'll create and format a report that shows order information by product category.

1. Open the SynthesisReportsDB database.
   From the current chapter folder, if necessary.
2. Create a report using the Report Wizard that includes the following fields from the following tables:
   - Categories: CategoryName
   - Categories: Picture
   - Orders: OrderDate
   - Products: ProductName
   - Customers: CompanyName
3. View the data by categories.
4. Order the report by OrderDate.
5. Use a Stepped layout with Landscape orientation.
6. Name the report Orders by Category and Customer.
7. Make the following control changes:
   - Make the OrderDate information appear to the left of the ProductName information.
   - Remove the CategoryName and Picture labels from the Page Header.
   - Widen or narrow columns in Layout view to improve the appearance of the report.
8. Add the `2000px-Report.png` image to the Page header, using the Clip size mode.
9. Filter the report to show only 2015 orders.
10. Print Preview the report and make any changes you like.
11. Save and close the report.

A sample of how the synthesis exercise report might look

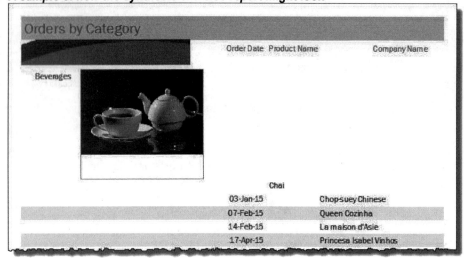